MILEY SPEAKS

A True Story of Love, Loss, Grief, and
Reconnection

Lisa Peachey and Carol Elizabeth Long

5D Garden LLC

This book is dedicated those who have gone before us, yet remain in our hearts.

Contents

INTRODUCTION

This morning, my husband Dene and I rushed our dog Sprout to the vet, fearing he'd had a stroke during the night. Although we don't know his exact age since he was already an adult when we adopted him, he's been with us for over twelve years, and age is undoubtedly catching up with him. Seeing him now—disoriented, confused, and wobbling around—is deeply alarming. We're holding onto hope that it might be something treatable and that with a little care, he'll soon return to his old self.

While waiting at the animal hospital, we met a woman who had just lost her dog a few days earlier. She was visibly struggling with grief, and I felt a strong urge to help her. I had a manifestation journal in the car—a project Elizabeth, Miley, and I created to guide others—and decided to give it to her. At the time, this journal included bonus material: excerpts from my early conversations with Miley, translated by animal communicator Elizabeth Long. As I handed it to her, I realized this wasn't the first time I had shared these transcripts with someone grieving the loss of a beloved pet or person. It struck me that these conversations might resonate even more deeply in a dedicated format.

This book is that format. Within these pages, I share the story of how Miley and Sprout entered my life and my heart, and the profound conversations that emerged after Miley's passing, as translated by Elizabeth Long.

CHAPTER ONE

Miley

In October 2006, Dene and I faced the heartbreaking loss of our beloved Akita, Keisha, to cancer. We had adopted him when he was about seven years old, and were blessed with six incredible years by his side.

Every day with him was a joy and a gift. We would have taken him everywhere if we could, but you can't exactly pop a ninety-five-pound Akita into your purse and bring them into a restaurant or a friend's house "Paris Hilton style." Each time we returned home, even before the car came to a complete stop, I'd say, "Keisha, we're home," knowing he'd already heard us and would be waiting at the door, as if nothing else mattered except us being together.

Keisha was more than a pet; he was my friend, confidant, and shadow, always nearby, quietly watching over me. When his health declined, we did everything we could, but ultimately, we had to make the heartbreaking decision to let him go.

After he was gone, coming home felt like a different world. Now when we rolled into the driveway, I'd turn to Dene and say, "We're home...no one cares." I cried every day—through the rest of October, November—every single day. Dene didn't talk about it, but he was hurting, too; I could see it in the way he'd throw himself into our work, or he'd mope around the house, lost and quiet, when we were home. We agreed that we never wanted to go through that kind of pain again, so we decided: no more dogs.

We had a cat named Luigi, who had been with me even longer than Dene. Luigi and I were pals, but he was the quintessential standoffish cat—everything was always on his terms. Petting, cuddling, lap time... and, well, pretty much everything else. I started teasing Luigi, telling him he needed to step up his game. At first, it was just a casual remark—an offhand comment that it was all up to him now and that he had some big shoes (or paws) to fill. But as the weeks went on, I found myself pleading with him to be more of a "lap kitty" to help me fill the void in my heart. I loved Luigi deeply, and we'd been through so much together over the years. I thought he'd understand and instinctively know what to do—to give me the comfort I so desperately needed. But it stung even more that he didn't even try to play the role, not even for a moment. He wouldn't so much as pretend to be more dog-like, and that hurt in ways I hadn't expected.

In December, Dene said he couldn't take it anymore—I was still crying every day, and Christmas loomed like an unwelcome guest. Dene pointed out that Luigi wasn't going to change, and maybe it was time to consider getting another dog, since I was clearly struggling without one. I agreed to think about it and started looking online about available adoptions on Petfinder. I also started talking to an Akita breeder in New Hampshire about a puppy, clearly falling into the trap of wanting to re-create Keisha.

Ultimately, though, getting another Akita was out of the question. When Keisha had his first seizure, Dene was away on business, and I was painfully reminded of my limitations. I simply couldn't manage getting a ninety-five-pound incapacitated dog into the car and to the vet on my own. I knew I never wanted to feel that helpless again. Beyond that, having a dog of Keisha's size came with unique considerations. Their strength and presence are part of what makes them so special. But that also means being mindful of the needs and the safety of others, which can sometimes pose challenges. On top of that, Dene and I had a business to run, and training a puppy didn't fit into our busy schedules. As tempting as it was to "find another Keisha," there were too many reasons why it wasn't the right choice for us.

Additionally, we both felt strongly about rescuing a dog. Knowing that thousands of dogs were waiting for a forever home, I focused my search on Petfinder.com. My parameters narrowed to adult dogs under fifty pounds.

The moment I saw Miley's picture, I was immediately captivated. Her gaze was magnetic, as if she could see straight into my soul. From that moment on, I couldn't think about any other dog. Something had shifted within me, and I immediately contacted the adoption agency. Miley—and her puppy, Prissy—had been rescued from a kill shelter in Tennessee and were now in foster care. Both desperately needed a forever home. Prissy was undeniably adorable, but Dene and I had already decided we didn't have the time or energy for a puppy. Besides, for me, there was already only Miley.

I was nervous because we had to commit to adopting Miley without meeting her in person before she could be sent to New England. I asked countless questions, but it wasn't the same as meeting her face-to-face. At one point, Dene said to me, "I support whatever you decide to do, but don't expect me to love this dog the way I loved Keisha." It felt like he was giving himself an easy out in case things didn't work out, leaving me to bear the full responsibility. I understood how big a commitment this was and kept dragging my feet—I didn't want to make the wrong decision.

One evening, while Dene and I were watching television, I was still agonizing over it. "What kind of name is Miley?" I asked aloud. Moments later, an advertisement came on for Miley Cyrus as *Hannah Montana*. I took it as a sign from the Universe and emailed the adoption agency to say we were ready to commit.

We arranged to pick her up at 7 a.m. on Saturday, December 30, 2006, at the Park & Ride off the interstate in

Plainfield, Connecticut—about a two-hour drive from our home on Cape Cod. The morning was cold and snowy, so we left extra early, allowing time for any delays. Despite the weather, we made excellent time and arrived early, with enough time to enjoy breakfast at a little diner just around the corner as we waited.

By 7 a.m., a small crowd had gathered at the Park & Ride lot, all there to meet the transport van. Among them was a young couple from Cape Cod who had adopted Miley's puppy, Prissy.

When the van pulled into the lot, the anticipation grew. It was a typical Ford cargo van, packed with stacked crates, each holding a dog. I remember it as if it were yesterday: the driver slid open the side door and began unloading dogs one by one, matching them with their new families.

Then I saw her. Miley was posed like a Sphinx inside a dingy mauve-colored crate, completely regal and serene. Her eyes locked with mine, and in that instant, I knew—this was our dog. I silently told her, *"You're coming home with us."*

Miley was the very last dog to come out of the van. The driver leashed her and led her out of the crate, cautioning, "Be careful; she's really strong." She handed me the leash, and just like that, Miley was ours.

We walked her around the parking lot a bit, letting her stretch her legs and settle in. For a small dog, she was surprisingly strong and powerful! Once she was ready, we settled her onto a dog bed in the back seat of our car and hit the road. She curled up in a little orange ball and slept the entire way home.

Arriving home with Miley was magical. We were still grieving Keisha, and the house felt like it belonged to his memory. Yet Miley strolled in as if she'd always been there, confidently claiming every corner as her own in a way that somehow felt right.

Dene was still trying to remain "loyal" to Keisha, holding back with Miley as if to protect his own heart. But that first night, she climbed onto the bed and wiggled her way into the middle, right between us. She nestled against Dene's arm, resting her head on his shoulder. In that moment, Miley stole his heart forever.

Miley settled in quickly, though we needed help with her and Luigi adjusting to each other, and she seemed to have no understanding of even the most basic commands. We brought in the same dog trainer who had helped us with Keisha. After spending time with Miley, the trainer informed us she was the second most challenging dog he'd ever encountered—her headstrong, stubborn nature and determination to have her way made every session a test of patience. In her private lessons, it was a constant battle of wills that might have been comical if it hadn't been so frustrating.

We all worked together on her training, dedicating countless hours to shaping her behavior. Years later, when people would comment, "She's so well-behaved; you're so lucky!" we'd just smile, knowing exactly how much effort had gone into that "luck."

When Miley first arrived, she was in rough physical shape. Much of her fur had fallen out, and she was painfully skinny, her ribs starkly visible. She smelled strongly of flea powder, urine, and kennel—a clear sign she was in desperate need of some TLC. We immediately began working with a groomer and introduced her to a proper, balanced diet. As she got cleaned up and her fur grew back, it transformed into a luxurious coat that shone with health and vitality. It was magnificent!

Miley filled the hole in our hearts after we lost Keisha. We still missed him deeply, but Miley brought a force all her own. She was entirely different from Keisha, yet she was everything we needed in her own unique way. Over time, she even learned to get along with Luigi, who tolerated her well enough until he passed away several years later at the impressive age of nineteen.

Keisha would always hold a special place in our hearts, but Miley brought a vibrant energy that healed us in a way only she could.

Miley in all of her glory

CHAPTER TWO

Sprout

By 2012, our business was thriving and growing rapidly, demanding more of our time and attention. When we first got Miley, I had been working from home, able to spend most of the day with her. But as the business expanded, my daily presence was needed at our location for long hours. With the landlord's strict no-dogs policy, we had no choice but to start leaving Miley at home alone.

Around this time, Miley developed hip problems, and our vet suggested she might be turning into a couch potato during our extended workdays. It was clear she could benefit from a companion to keep her company and encourage her to stay active. And so, we decided it was time to find her a friend.

In June 2012, I returned to Petfinder and found myself drawn to a little dog named "Napoleon." He was at a shelter in Rhode Island, just a few hours away. I took the day off, packed up Miley, and we set out to meet him.

Napoleon had been at the shelter for over a month, and I couldn't understand why. Little dogs like him were usually adopted quickly, and he was so cute—it just didn't make sense. The staff explained that he'd originally been picked up as a stray and adopted once before, but he was returned because he was "mouthy." This time, they were determined to find him a home with another dog to keep him engaged.

Miley and Napoleon seemed to hit it off right away, and I was completely charmed by his quirky personality. Without hesitation, I completed the adoption paperwork and brought him home. The drive back was anything but smooth—he was sick the entire way—and when we arrived home, he immediately bit Dene. We were definitely not off to a good start.

"Napoleon" felt like a name with too many negative connotations, and since he didn't seem to respond to it anyway, we decided to rename him. It was Dene's idea to call him Sprout, inspired by the Jolly Green Giant's little friend from the vegetable commercials. Sprout was playful, optimistic, and eager to learn—qualities that made the name a perfect fit for a dog who clearly needed a fresh start.

I adored Sprout from the beginning, though it was clear he had issues with men. Dene, ever patient, slowly built trust with him, and after a couple of years, they became the best of buddies.

At first, Miley seemed bemused—or perhaps annoyed—by Sprout's boundless energy. Soon enough, though, she asserted herself and showed him who was boss. Watching them together, I could see her lightening up in ways I hadn't expected.

While we initially got Sprout for Miley's benefit, it didn't take long for the four of us to become a family—with Miley firmly in charge. Our years together were exceptional. We got an RV and took Miley and Sprout on vacations, exploring the East Coast together.

When I became environmentally ill with chemical sensitivity, Miley was my rock. After long days of medical treatments, she'd throw herself down next to me—or sometimes right on top of me—and somehow, I'd feel better. Later, as Dene had to travel more frequently to

California to support his aging father, I always felt safe at home with Miley by my side and Sprout ever alert to anything happening in the house. Together, they made sure I was never lonely or afraid.

Sprout brought a spark of new energy into our home, filling it with laughter and joy. Miley, always the serious one, began to show a lighter side with him around, a change that lifted all of our spirits. For a while, I couldn't have imagined our little family any other way. Life felt whole and perfectly balanced, with each of us bringing something special to the other.

Sprout—the quirky little guy who unexpectedly stole our hearts.

CHAPTER THREE

Losing Miley

In early 2020, Miley's health began to deteriorate. We did everything we could to keep her comfortable and mobile. Initially, acupuncture and chiropractic adjustments worked wonders. Later, anti-inflammatory and pain medications helped for a while. But as the months went on, her mobility worsened—she struggled to walk, became increasingly incontinent (which clearly distressed her more than it did us), and eventually couldn't stand on her own.

We knew we were nearing the end of Miley's life, and the decision we faced weighed heavily on us. I prayed for her to pass peacefully in her sleep, sparing us the agonizing choice. But each day, I begged God, The Universe, anyone who would listen, *please just don't let today be that day.* It felt just like it had with Keisha. The guilt of waiting too long with him still haunted us. Here we were again, facing the same heartbreaking decision. It was emotional torture.

Then COVID happened, and suddenly, regular access to veterinary care, acupuncture, and chiropractic treatments for Miley became unreliable. Our vet implemented a drop-off-only policy for all pet appointments, including euthanasia. Miley's acupuncturist, Dr. M, who was also a veterinarian and had always come to the house, offered the compassionate service of in-home euthanasia. By December 2020, Miley was visibly struggling to get through each day. She was so unflappable, so stoic—our little soldier—that it was hard to gauge just how much pain she might have been enduring.

One thing was certain: we would not let her pass alone in a vet's office. Dr. M was able to schedule an at-home euthanasia. We knew if we waited and Dr. M contracted COVID or had to quarantine, we'd be forced into the drop-off situation at the vet's office, leaving Miley to cross over by herself. That was simply unacceptable. Reluctantly, we set the date: Dr. M would come to our house for Friday, December 11th, at 11 a.m.

The days leading up to it were filled with love and care. We did everything we could to make Miley comfortable and gave her as much attention as she'd let us, cherishing each moment with her.

Early that Friday morning, Dene had a quick appointment with the chiropractor. While he was there, he spoke about our struggle with the euthanasia scheduled for Miley later that morning. Another patient overheard him and said, "I know someone who might be able to help you," handing him the contact information for Elizabeth Long. It felt like fate—Dene hadn't even planned to mention Miley's situation, but that one conversation changed everything.

As soon as Dene got home, we reached out to Elizabeth, hoping for an emergency communication session with Miley. The soonest she could fit us in was the following week. We wanted to ask Miley if this was the right choice, and suddenly we faced the decision of whether to postpone the appointment with Dr. M. However, Dr. M was booked out for another two weeks, and with COVID restrictions still a factor, waiting carried risks. Miley was also declining by the day. Elizabeth assured us that she could still connect with Miley after she passed, so with heavy hearts, we decided to keep our appointment with Dr. M for that day.

December 11th was a beautiful, sunny day on Cape Cod—not too cold. Dene and I took Miley for one last visit to the beach. He carried her to the sand, and she lay quietly, watching the waves roll in. The sky was a brilliant blue, with puffy white clouds drifting over the ocean, and the sun sparkled across the water. The air was crisp and clean. It was peaceful, beautiful—a perfect farewell. I captured a few photos of her that day, never imagining then that one would become the cover of her book.

Shortly after we returned home, Dr. M arrived. We made Miley comfortable and let her indulge in as much liver pâté as she wanted—her absolute favorite. Dene, Sprout, and I sat with her, holding her as she crossed over, and once again, our hearts were broken.

Our grief was profound; the three of us felt lost without her. The following days passed in a blur of heartache, but we clung to the hope of our appointment with Elizabeth. We needed to know if we had made the right choice, and we also needed guidance on how to help Sprout, who was struggling without his friend.

Losing Miley was shattering. Her presence had been woven into every aspect of my life, and in her absence, I struggled to grasp how anything could fill the void she left. But as the initial shock began to subside, I found myself starting to feel her in unexpected ways. The depth of our bond, as I began to realize, wasn't solely tied to her physical presence.

Miley felt close, as though she was gently reminding me that our connection could transcend the physical. I would soon learn through our sessions that love, intention, and attention are powerful forces—ones that connect us across any boundary. Her departure had taught me not only about loss but also about an enduring closeness that would continue to unfold. This deeper connection, one that I had never fully understood before, would become a guiding light as I moved forward.

With no real idea of what to expect, we placed our trust—and our broken hearts—in the hands of a woman we had never met and had only briefly spoken to on the phone on one of the hardest days of our lives.

Little did we know, Miley's departure would upend our understanding of reality and mark the beginning of something extraordinary.

Miley's last day...

CHAPTER FOUR

Elizabeth

I first connected with Miley shortly after she transitioned. It was like she had been waiting with her talking points all her life. She was incredibly organized and able to track all that she wanted to deliver. Like many animals, she knew every note of the songs in the hearts of her humans; those vibrational melodies that make up the uniqueness of each of us. She proceeded to dive into rearranging the score into a higher octave of well-being for Lisa and Dene, and she continues to do that to this day.

Miley serves as narrator, teacher, guide, and nurturer in these sessions. She coagulates and relays information from a variety of spiritual sources: Archangels, Teachers of Light, Ascended Masters, Elohim, the Fae, as well as Lisa, Dene, and my own spiritual guides. Conversations with animals involve translation, and the results of that render written or even spoken words that sound different than normal human-to-human conversation. The frequency of what the animal sends is translated into written words, and in order to convey as much of the frequency as possible, punctuation and grammar are unique.

The process of translating information into the linear human language of words is unique for every animal communicator, and the result here is a transcript that sounds slightly different from human-to-human translation. Grammar, word flow, and punctuation are unique. For instance, you'll find more commas; they indicate a pause. During the back-and-forth rhythm of conversation, the animal sometimes has to wait for me to move my attention to the place they want to address. They pause to make sure I'm connected to the energy they want to show us, but also to place emphasis on what they are about to say or show.

I was impressed with the force of energy from Lisa and Dene when they first called me a few hours before their heart-wrenching decision to free Miley's spirit from her aging body. Dene spoke to me first. He was extremely emotional; even describing this now brings tears to my eyes at how evident his love for her was. He was completely devoted, torn about how to give her what she wanted, and in pain around his own impending loss. I did my best to help him understand what I had learned from my experiences with many humans and animals in this situation. Then he handed the phone to Lisa, whose approach was to manage everything in detail to give Miley what she needed at that moment. Between the three of us, and likely Miley herself, I later realized, we were able to navigate launching Miley across her River Styx, ensuring she could truly rest in peace.

A few days later, I connected with her for our first session. Obviously, the riverboat ride and rest had gone well, as she was fully prepared and able to converse.

CHAPTER FIVE

December 14: Miley's 1st Session-Three Days Since Miley Passed

I barely remember anything from Friday afternoon after Miley passed until Monday, when we received the first session transcript. All I know is that I felt numb—devastated, barely functioning-I'm not sure if I even left the house. Dene, Sprout, and I drifted through those days like ghosts, trapped in a fog of loss, barely going through the motions. Looking back, it's as if those days barely existed at all.

Somewhere in that haze, we began preparing for Elizabeth's communication with Miley—and with Sprout, since we also needed to know if he was okay. We had no idea what to expect or how to prepare, let alone what questions to ask. Elizabeth instructed us to send photos of Miley and Sprout—one where they're looking at the camera with eyes open—and to write a series of questions for each of them, addressing the questions as if speaking directly to them. Dene and I spent a lot of time discussing it and drafted some questions. When we sent them to Elizabeth, she replied, asking for clarification on a few points. Elizabeth's guidance here was invaluable as we had no clue what was about to happen.

We knew which day Elizabeth would conduct the sessions but not the exact time or what, if anything, we were supposed to do. Elizabeth advised us to let Sprout go about his day as usual, avoiding any stress or disruptions, such as a vet visit. So we watched him and waited, wondering if we'd be able to sense when he was communicating with her. But, with Sprout sleeping most of the time, there were no visible clues.

We'd always believed Miley and Sprout were smart and loving beings, but we had never experienced animal communication before. We were completely unprepared for what was about to happen.

It's important to note that we were not present during Elizabeth's communication with Miley and Sprout. Each transcript arrived all at once after the sessions were complete, just as you are about to see them. We had no chance to change or refine the questions in response to how things were going. And what unfolded was so utterly unexpected, so profoundly surprising, that we were stunned. Already emotionally wrecked, we hadn't anticipated Miley's voice and personality coming through so vividly, and with such clarity and conviction that it left us in awe.

Her words and energy were a gift—a light in our darkest days. I'm not sure what I was expecting, but it was definitely not this.

Email arrives from Elizabeth:

Hi Lisa and Dene,

Miley is doing fine; she is a very large, smart, evolved spirit in that dog body. She definitely plans to return. I think her messages are pretty clear.

Elizabeth

Miley session starts:

Miley feels very big to me now, in spirit, even as I just begin to set up. I see your spirit energies Dene and Lisa, quiet, observing. I call Miley.

E: Welcome Miley. You feel rich, solid, strong and very encompassing in spirit, now.

M: I am a wise Being, in body, and now in spirit, yes. I am very relieved to have flowed successfully through the gate of transition. However, there was much...(she shows me 'stickiness')...wavering in my leaving. I hesitated, wishing to continue to provide stability, afraid my absence would destabilize the family.

E: I understand, Miley - I see the power and grounding energy that you hold. Your family has many questions and messages; it is evident you were such a large part of their lives. In order to be able to convey all of the messages to you, I may send you several in batches, and you can choose which to respond to and show us what you need to. But first I want to ask you to tell us what you think is important, and show us how you are now.

M: I, AM FINE. Please do not use your energy in concern for me. I came to care for you, in a way that humans do not care for each other. I came to teach you, and I am not done yet. Fear not, I will complete this mission. (she is very absolute in her energy around this)

E: Miley, I think that is one of Lisa's questions - she believes you will return.

M: And I will. She knows that. There will be a time of becoming ready on both sides, but in a flash I will be home, then.

E: I believe you will - you are very powerful, Miley. Your confidence/mastery energy is amazing, comforting even to me. May I give you some messages from Lisa and Dene?

M: Of course.

E: (she has such a strong sense of family with you - different from a lot of relationships I see) Lisa says, "First of all I want to tell you how much I love you and miss you already. When you came into my life you healed my broken heart after the loss of Keisha. You have been my friend and my child for all of these years and I want you to know how truly grateful I am. I want you to know that there have been times in moments of darkness when you have saved me, really saved my life."

32   MILEY SPEAKS

M: That commitment from me remains, and continues (very solemn, like a vow).

E: Lisa continues: "I want you to know that I am ok, because I really believe in YOU. I know that you are strong and beautiful, and the path forward for you is full of adventure and love. I know in my heart that you are ok and I don't want to hold you back and I don't want you to worry about us. We are sad because we miss you and it is as if someone turned the lights down at home with you gone. But we will adjust and be ok knowing that you are starting a new chapter."

M: (she pulls this in strongly, her energy flickers at the lights down) I can turn them up. I can hold the light for you. That is not taxing, not prohibitive for what I need to pass through, now, at all.

E: I know that Lisa and Dene would not want you to use any energy you need now, Miley.

M: I will hold a light in the home. I can come tonight, your 'tonight'.

E: You are strong in your certainty, Miley. Thank you - and only if it is of no prohibitive impact on you.

M: (looks directly at me - she would not compromise herself) Of course. And it is part of my mission, still.

E: Do you want to be any more explicit about your ongoing mission? Please tell us more about that or we can go to more questions.

M: Questions, please. (shows me her shifting her body, moving forward, closer)

E: "Did you have enough time? We were worried that we transitioned you too soon or that we waited too long?"

M: Overall, we are not finished and I will return (she looks at me quizzically re the 'time' question).

E: And at the end, Miley? You showed us first thing that it was difficult to leave - was the timing ok for you?

M: Yes. I could have left sooner, but it is of no consequence - my job was to care for you in a specific way, and I am doing that, did that, will do that. (she shows me a wide umbrella of caring for you, extending backward and forward along the timeline)

E: "Can you hear us when we talk to you?"

M: Of course (she sends laughing sounds, chuckle energy). I am with you. I do not respond, as I am holding a more neutral space, in order to process. But if you need me I will know, and I will come, with energy, immediately to assist you. Guiding you in spirit is part of my commitment.

E: I know they would want you to prioritize yourself.

M: (she looks at me keenly) They ARE my priority. When I prioritize my family, I AM prioritizing myself.

E: Lisa wants to know: "Is there anything you would like us to do for you? Do you have any idea when we will be together again? Will it be on the other side or will you be coming back here again first?"

M: We are not done yet with Earth school. I am eager to return. Yet I must walk through this process as I unfold myself. You see I folded my Beingness up very tight to compress it into a small canine body. I may choose a lighter, springier body, this time, so as to bring in the energies of the air elemental more, even water - to flow more information through our lives. (to you Lisa) Study hard (she's sending humor), so we can start at a more advanced level this time.

E: You are showing me you do need some time to process. Is the 'study hard' - what you'd like Lisa and Dene to do for you?

M: Yes indeed. Dig into your inner selves, learn what you can, know yourself more so that when I return, I can bring MORE of my spiritual energy into my body, matching yours.

E: Wonderful instructions, Miley. You know Lisa has some questions of sweetness for you: "Were you happy with us?"

M: There was no unhappiness - there is no comparison. I am more of a Being who relishes vibrancy. That is my happiness. So the answer to your question is Extremely.

E: "What was your favorite thing to do other than eat treats? What did you think when we called you Mini Pup or Mini? Did you love us and did you love Sprout?"

M: (more humor dancing through her energy field) I loved Sprout and you both with all my heart. Did it look that way, that you ask? I gave you all, each, individually what you needed, though the pictures of that might not match what many would call 'love'. It was more than that…

E: Mini-pup?

M: An inversion of my large beingness. Sometimes funny. Sometimes slightly irritated. I would like a larger body.

E: Got it - you are funny, even in your seriousness, Miley. Lisa says, "I love you and miss you and will always have you in my heart. Thank you for being in my life and making my life better."

M: (looks at you) We are just getting started. As I move through this space of 'neutral', and you move through your space of 'missingness', we will begin to connect more avidly (she chooses that word), and start the process of aligning energies for a higher vibration match in our reunification in the physical. (she rests as I begin to flow to her that I am bringing in Dene's questions, her gaze is towards your energy, Lisa, breathing more slowly but deeply) Lisa, breathe. Relax, you will hear me, at times. Know that we are aligning. You will not get this alignment, this path, wrong.

E: Thank you, Miley. That is always a human concern. Will you hear from Dene, now?

M: Of course. (she shifts her energy - she has a markedly different connection for your energy, Dene - not greater or lesser, just different).

E: He says, as he begins, "The truth is I miss you terribly and cry several times a day. But I'll be OK. I love you and will love and miss you forever. You are my best friend and I am sorry to part with you. I hope I didn't keep you too long."

M: And I know this, and I have sent gentle flowings of connectedness, still, to you, because I know this is what you need. I can do that, as long as you need it. (I see that she is loving to assist in this way, as it works for you, and shows me immediately that it works, for her, as well)

E: Thank you, Miley. Here are more of Dene's questions and messages. "I am worried about Sprout, Miley can you talk to Sprout and help him deal with you not being here? Please encourage him to be strong and be at peace. Let him know we love him too!"

M: Sprout is a project, and I will work with him.

E: "You seemed to like going places. Did you have a favorite place? You seemed happiest when all the extended family got together and you were there. Is that right?"

M: I am an excellent Commander, and yes I was in my joy with many to command, who all loved me, and respected me even more.

E: He wonders about the last of your time: "Did you suffer, were you in pain? Did I keep you too long? It was so very hard for me to know the right time. I love you, if I hurt or offended you I'm sorry, please forgive me. I thank you for your forgiveness. I feel so guilty about not telling you in advance what was going to happen on the day we set you free from your body, but I didn't really know how to. Please forgive me, my friend."

M: I am a powerful being, and still I am who you loved so, Dene. (she sends this very tenderly) I was already leaving, one toe of spirit in the body, waiting, finding the right time to step out. You helped me make that step, and I am very grateful. Your heart is pure in the feelings you flow to me, and I know that. Pure. It is perfect, in a world of imperfection, your heart. I can touch you through your heart, still. Do not wince - I will wait until you are in strength and can receive my touch.

E: "How was your last day with us? Was the drive with you on my lap and the window down fun? Was the beach nice for you? I wanted you to be surrounded by beauty and love. You seemed relaxed when I carried you up and down the stairs. I hope I did OK and didn't hurt you."

M: It was an imprint - of our times together on this beautiful adventurous planet Earth, yes, Dene: You did exactly as I would have wished, it felt like...(she looks for an analogy) A song, to me. A song of sweetness. (she stops, is caught in the emotion for a moment) Take me there, when you find me, again please.

E: :"How are you now? I imagine you can run "90 Miley's per hour!" Can you describe where you are at and /or what it's like there? Do you feel happy and safe? Have you met any of my friends or nice other beings where you are and have they been helpful?"

M: I am in stasis, neutral, processing my time with you in that body. That somewhat solitary process has my attention. And I am watching you, withdrawing the focus that I need to, from Earth, slowly. That is the way to do it elegantly, you see. Death, as it is called, is not simply the 'lights out' moment, it is a longer process of returning, and turning back, and returning with more (energy, she shows me). It is more of a weaving process, loosening some threads, pulling tighter others: A dance of sorts as well.

E: "Did you know I was singing to you all those times? Did you understand when I told you I love you all those times? Did you feel loved with my songs?"

M: You nurtured me, Dene, in your own unique way, you did. Your creativity in expressing your love was mesmerizing, and still is. You put your heart out front, and trip all over yourself coming behind it as you catch up, and it is quite beautiful. I love both of you, when I feel your hearts, and feel this language.

E: "How did you feel about your nicknames like Mini Pups, Mile-Zo and furry baby pup? I know you are a full grown adult dog, but I enjoyed thinking of you as my little baby. I hope you didn't mind. We were early morning buddies and I'm glad you were with me. It was great starting my morning with you, thanks."

M: I know you are 'silly' in your love, in your nurturing. It was quite freeing to me, to be able to let go and let you baby me for a moment. I accepted it, as I accept Lisa's love, and Sprouts' love - it is all different, and luscious.

E: "I believe in you my friend and know you can do whatever you need to progress and I wish you all the best. Is there anything you want me to know? Can I contact you directly? Through dreams or meditation?"

M: When you are ready, call to me - as your friend, simply, easily. We have different contracts - my contract with Lisa is different from my contract with you, and even with Sprout. Our relationships grow out of these structures, and are different, and beautiful, and inter-weave into the beauty that is our family, still....

E: "For some reason, I feel I have friends in your dimension now and I have asked them to help you if they can and if you accept. I just pray for your well being my friend and if our paths ever cross again it will be a good day for me. You are the greatest mini pup in the universe and you were perfect for me! I love you. Please be happy and filled with joy and peace."

M: Thank you, Dene, for your offering. (very solemn, now)I feel your gift of joy, and I may be able to share and laugh with love for you, with your friends. And yes, our paths will cross. You may hold yourself, and wait to decide - is it me, really me? And I will laugh at and with you, and in joy, when you know. You will know. Then take me to the beach, you see; that is the time, the sealing.

E: Thank you, Miley. Do you have anything else to say? I will go to Sprout soon - he needs help. If you wish to witness, and assist while I am with Sprout, please do with your wisdom. I will set him in some alignment for a bit, that's a good space if you wish to assist, and he wants that as well.

M: Yes. I am complete.

Session ends.

Elizabeth

LISA'S REACTION:

I cannot begin to express how deeply Miley's words eased my pain, after believing she was gone from my life forever. No—not just her words, the *connection*. Miley was no longer lost to me forever. Her session took place on Monday, December 14th, just three days after her passing. We were still drowning in grief and had no idea what to expect from these sessions. We could never have anticipated a comprehensive dialogue with this complex, multidimensional being—a sentient soul who, until recently, had shared our home in a dog's body.

This was Miley in every way I had known her, comforting us, even when I thought it was our role to ensure she was at peace and transitioning safely, moving into the light...or whatever awaited her. Instead, she was healing us—something I had not anticipated but desperately needed.

When Miley shared, "I was afraid my absence would destabilize the family environment," her words struck me to my core, revealing just how deeply she understood our family dynamics. There's no question in my mind that, at times, Miley and Sprout were the glue that held us together. As a husband and wife team running a business and dealing with my chronic, incapacitating illness over many years, Dene and I were regularly under intense stress. Our relationship was often pushed to its limits, and I have no doubt that Miley and Sprout were instrumental in keeping our family grounded and whole.

Miley promised, *"I will hold a light in the home. I can come tonight."* We had been struggling so deeply with her loss, especially Dene, who seemed burdened by a profound darkness. That night, after the session, Dene felt her presence come to him—And a light ignited in his spirit, lifting the immense weight he had been carrying and allowing him to begin healing for the first time since her passing.

And then there was "Mini-pup." We had so many pet names for Miley, but "Mini-pup" was the most frequent—our way of endearingly acknowledging her as a miniature big dog. I often told Dene, 'I think she's annoyed when I call her Mini. I can almost hear her saying, "I'm not Mini; I am MIGHTY!"' Now, it all makes sense to me. The memory makes me smile and brings tears to my eyes. Miley was, indeed, a complex and powerful soul, yet we lovingly addressed her as "Mini-pup" and "Mini-baby" for years because of her unique, adorable form. Looking back, I can see that the universe has a sense of humor—and apparently, so does Miley.

CHAPTER SIX

December 14: Sprout's 1st Session

Email arrives from Elizabeth:

Sprout was really disorganized and out of alignment and clearly needed help; so when I connected with him, I helped him align and rest in that for a little while, then came back to him. When I returned after a break, he was more aligned and I saw his energy as clear, rather than like looking at two or three old photo negatives that don't line up. And he was and is eager to shift and change, as he can. He is going through a lot right now. When I started into subjects of his inappropriate peeing and his past, he backed way into 'bad dog'; into a past state of being abused. This was too much for him at one time, especially being the first time we've connected, right after losing Miley. I pulled away from those subjects making it clear that he is not a 'bad dog', and went to the messages of appreciation for him. I did mention getting another dog, and he thinks maybe later, not right now. He really has his plate full with the adjustment he is going through.

Elizabeth

Sprout session starts:

Sprout first sends me, as I am connecting with him, 'Where am I? Where is Miley?' He shows me that he is a little confused about life with/without a body, even to the degree where he wonders why he still has his body - he can sense Miley's energy out of her body, and he is looking to see if he is out of his body too.

E: Sprout?

S: I am here but where is here?

E: Sprout, I see your confusion, and I have been asked by Lisa and Dene, and Miley to show you how things are stabilizing, now. I know it was a tremendous shift for everyone when Miley left her body, and went to her spirit body only now.

S: But where is her body? Is it waiting for her? Will she come back to it?

E: No, she will not, Sprout, and I see that you actually have knowledge of that process in your own memory banks somewhere - I think you are in a little bit of shock, a jolt, a space of not really knowing everything that you normally know because of the suddenness of this event. Can you breathe with me, and let that sync you into alignment, out of the trauma?

S: I am trying to not 'trauma'.

E: It's not really a good or bad thing, Sprout, and it's ok if you are in that space - it's sometimes part of the process of events and life. I think you know this. You're just a little bit knocked out of your body right now.

S: More than a little!

E: And that's alright. Lisa and Dene would like to help you adjust, and align with the new family structure in the body, now. Would you like to breathe with me?

S: Yes. (kinda comes out of nowhere, a willingness)

E: Alright, let's breathe together (he shows me his intense eyes, connecting).

S: Miley was my buffer. She did everything. I have been small in spirit and she accepted that, even relished that (he shows a slight perturbance in the 'relish').

E: Sprout, you have had an interesting relationship with Miley, and a somewhat turbulent early life. I think we can help you align today. I am going to give you some time to breathe in this space of healing and connection. I will take a little break, and then return to talk with you - is that ok?

S: Yes. (firmly, and breathing)

E: Archangel Michael will stay with you, connecting you to the healing energy of the Earth more fully.

S: I see Miley.

E: Yes (I'm laughing, he's funny) She is there, too.

S: Thank you.

Break

Sprout: I'm here. (he immediately jumps forward)I'm better now. Thank you. I don't want to be a problem. It's just confusing.

E: We understand, Sprout. Lisa and Dene are concerned and want to help you with anything they can. They are adjusting as well.

S: I know I could be helping them but my own self is here (he shows me the off-balance, trying to adjust).

E: Would you like to hear their messages to you?

S: For me? Yes.

E: Lisa is talking, sending me the words, and Dene says that these are his messages too, so this is from both of them, even if you hear Lisa talking.

S: Ok. I love Lisa. I love Dene too. It's just different. They both love me but I'm inferior?

E: No, not inferior, just different. We are all different.

S: Ok. (he seems willing to accept that).

E: Here is the first message, "First I want to tell you how much I love you and how grateful I am to have you in my life. You make every day better just by being there. You have also helped Grandma immensely since she got sick with Alzheimer's and that has been very special."

S: I'm good with that! I can do that!

E: I bet you can. You can be very present, Sprout, from what I see.

S: She loves me.

E: I'm sure. So more messages, "I know that it is going to be lonely with Miley gone and I want to know what we can do to help you adjust. I will try to bring you with me and also have Dene bring you with him to more places so that you are not home alone a lot."

S: I would like that.

E: Now, this is an important subject, and it's a little different from the other messages - it's a request for a behavior change. Do you want to talk about this now, or would you like to hear some other messages first, Sprout?

S: Oh. Um, oh. I want to hear other messages but now I'm worried. Did I do something bad? Yes I did something bad.

E: I think we need to remove 'bad' from our heartspace, and I will tell you what the request is now. We can talk about anything that comes up in our back and forth that might be part of this, but here is the request: "In return I would ask you to please not pee on or mark indoors anywhere or in anyone's house that I bring you. That is the way to be a good guest even though I know it goes against doggie nature. Please do this for me so that I can help you."

S: I already know it's bad. I can't help it. I'm sorry. I'm not good at this.

E: Sprout, let's find out how we can help you be successful. I'm going to read a message about before, before you were with Dene and Lisa, and let's see if there's anything there that can help us help you, ok?

S: Ok (he's shifting his weight back and forth from left to right).

E: Try to keep breathing into that relaxed space that we used to help you align, ok? You're not going to be held as a 'bad dog', we just want to open this box of how to help you move into a space of success with requests, ok?

S: Ok. That's better. No bad dogs.

E: Here is the message: "I suspect that you have had some hard times in the past before you came to us. It would help Dene and I understand why you get testy with us sometimes...

S: "Bad Dog!"

E: Sprout, were you called, even yelled at, 'Bad Dog', in the past?

S: It's all I ever heard.

E: What happened in the past? Lisa says, "Why do you shake sometimes when I put you in the car and what can I do to help you?"

S: It's cold, really cold, and bad dogs have to stay in the shed. (he shows me some kind of unheated building - could be a small separate garage)

E: What about the car?

S: And the car. They get left in the car for a long time - all night. And then they get hit for peeing in the car.

E: Sprout, that behavior was not about a dog, not about you; it was the behavior of a human who did not do things the way that person should have, for some reason. It is NOT what the majority of humans think is appropriate for dogs, and it really has nothing to do with you.

S: Yes it did, I was mad. I didn't like it.

E: That's a powerful response, Sprout.

S: That was me. (He shows me a little bit of pride in 'fighting back'.)

E: Sprout, Lisa has questions about this, maybe - just tell us what fighting back is.

S: Keeping boundaries. Hands sometimes hit. (he shows me he also notices if humans become absent minded or begin to dissociate....that this is warning behavior for him that he might get hit, or even if attention wanders while snuggling. He is showing me male hands)

E: I'm going to read you what Lisa says: "I know that you don't really want to bite Dene and me, and wonder why it gets to that point so fast sometimes. Dene wants

so much for you two to be best friends and I know sometimes you are friends because you sit with him on the sofa
a lot and snuggle with him in bed. But then you growl
at him when he picks you up to hold you to show you
that he loves you and we don't know why. Please tell us
how to help you. I do want you to know that we have
certainly noticed how much improvement there has been
since you have been with us. You have come a long way
and we know this and know it has not been easy. We
are very proud of you." Do you see this, Sprout? (it's a
lot for him -the request not to pee inappropriately, the
adjustment to Miley's absence, and bringing up his past).

S: I know it.

E: I think we're maybe talking about too many things
at once, today, Sprout. Let's reframe - Lisa and Dene notice how much progress you've made since you've been
with them, and they are very pleased and admire you
for helping Grandma. They want to help you adjust to
Miley's absence, and they understand that there are some
things that happened in your past that have caused you
to have certain behaviors now that everyone would like
for you to be able to let go of. So I can tell you some

more messages about some of these things, but I don't want your eyes to glaze over and have you back away in confusion, so please help find out what is ok to discuss now.

S: I love Grandma. I want to be only a good dog.

E: Lisa wants to explain something about seeing Grandma: "There is a sickness that is causing all of the humans to not spend time together until everyone gets vaccinated (Covid). So we don't see anyone much right now and that includes all of your extended pack and Grandma and Duke. But they still love you and ask about you and we will try to find ways to see them more soon, but will definitely see them more after the virus goes away."

S: Oh.

E: It doesn't have anything to do with you, Sprout. It's a human condition thing, and by the time the weather gets colder, then maybe a little warmer again, I bet you'll be able to see them again.

S: Ok. (he appreciates understanding this)

E: Lisa has a message of appreciation for you; you've helped Grandma, and Lisa also wants to tell you how you've helped Lisa: "I want you to know how important you are to me. When I have been sick or in pain you have always been there for me. When I am sad or lonely you are there for me. No matter how hard things get, you are always there for me and I want you to know how much that means to me and know that I love you and will always be there for you too."

S: (he softens, and moves forward again, towards me) I can do more of that too.

E: I bet you can, in fact I know you can, and that would be appreciated, Sprout. You have unique caring skills, I see, in how you help humans.

S: It's not so complicated.

E: It's not, is it? You know Miley was quite a complex Being.

S: I'm not. She was blindingly complex (he shows me this).

E: She had a certain kind of bright light, still does.

S: I know. I can see her light, I just can't see her.

E: Her body?

S: Yes. Oh, she's not here, in her body. I forgot for a minute.

E: That's ok. It was a big event, and I know you and Lisa and Dene are adjusting, and you will be for some time. We want to know what you need in order to adjust to not having Miley's body around.

S: Some time? But extra treats. (he shows me he wants to sleep if you leave him at home alone).

E: Are you good at deciding to take a nap and then doing it, Sprout?

S: Yes. SHORT naps.

E: Ok, I will advise Lisa and Dene that it will work best for you if they only leave you at home for short periods of time, ok?

S: Yes please.

E: Is there anything else you can think of that would help you adjust to Miley's absence? Dene asked, "Does it help you for us to keep Miley's bed and things around or do you not need that?"

S: Where will she sit when she comes with her light?

E: Do you see Miley's light in a form, or shape, Sprout?

S: I've seen it twice. She did sit in her bed once - the light. It's (he shows me like a blobby type dog shape).

E: I see. So should Dene and Lisa leave her bed out for awhile?

S: Don't you think that's a good idea?

E: Sure. They can leave it out for a while, and then maybe when you feel a little less tender about things changing so quickly, it can go away.

S: I think that's a good idea!

E: Sprout, I see that you have a lot of adjusting to do, not only to Miley's physical presence gone, but to handling some of the old stuff we brought up briefly. I'm sorry if mentioning it was too much; we absolutely do not have to talk about that right now - Lisa and Dene will ALWAYS take care of you - Lisa asked that, "Do you know that we will always take care of you?" Are you clear on that?

S: Yes I am. The old stuff is in my cells. We don't have to talk about it.

E: Ok, and we can help you when you're ready, alright? Just know that there is no bad dog.

S: Ok.

E: That's a real good simple starting point.

S: It feels good.

E: It does, doesn't it? Lisa had something she was wondering about...if it's too much to think about, just say 'Later', and they will ask you about it later, ok?

S: What is it?

E: They wonder, "Do you think you are going to be able to adjust to being the only dog in the house or do you need a friend?"

S: Another dog?

E: That's what they're wondering - but it's up to you.

S: Can I have some time to adjust first?

E: Of course.

S: I might think it's a good idea; I just don't know right now.

E: You need some time, we understand, Sprout. I have a message from Dene: "I love you Sprout and I promise to be your friend. I know things can get tense sometimes but let's just be really nice to each other. I won't hurt you. I love you. Can you please trust me and not be so growly with me?"

S: That's the bad dog.

E: It is that stuff from your past, Sprout. Dene doesn't think it's a big deal, but he'd really prefer it if you didn't mix him up with some other person from your past.

S: Is that what happens?

E: Yes, I think so. Dene can practice being focused with you - that's something humans usually relax when they're with sweet dogs like you, they relax their focus, they drift a little.

S: It feels scary.

E: We can ask Dene to be very present with you, to learn to relax and be present at the same time. Then maybe you won't get him mixed up with anyone from your past.

S: I don't want to talk about my past please.

E: Maybe we find some other way to take it out of your cellular memory, Sprout, so that it doesn't exist anymore.

S: I would like that.

E: I'll mention that to Lisa and Dene. Sprout, Here is the feeling that Lisa and Dene hope you can move into, as you go through your adjustment process. (I show him calm, relaxed, sense of fun, warmth, love, giving, feeling safe, grounded. He starts to pull that toward him, letting it flow into him). That is a good place to start.

S: It feels good, heh heh.

E: It does! Thank you for sharing that with me, Sprout. I'm going to leave you with that, and ask Lisa and Dene to flow all those good feelings to you.

S: I would like that.

E: They'll show you, and you can practice being that way yourself, flowing back to them.

S: I can do that.

E: Excellent. Do you have any more questions you'd like to ask, or anything you'd like to say today?

S: I feel ashamed (he shows me this) when I've looked like a bad dog. I'd like to not be that way.

E: I know they know that. They'll continue to help you out of those behaviors when you are ready, and I think that will come soon enough; right now there is a lot in front of you in terms of adjustment.

S: Yes there sure is.

E: And you're doing well, already, Sprout.

S: I am? (question/statement both)

E: Yes, you are. I see you moving towards a place where you are not as confused, and happier. It's not so complicated.

S: No, it's not.

E: So I will step back and disconnect now, if that's ok with you.

S: It's alright. Thank you. (he is so soft and sweet)

E: Then, bye for now, Sprout.

Session ends.

Elizabeth

LISA'S REACTION:

Sprout's session was a knife in my heart. Hearing his little voice just days after losing Miley was a shock—it was so completely Sprout, a reminder of his unique spirit, yet filled with the sorrow and confusion he was enduring. I was struck by how much he, too, was grieving Miley, and I was terrified realizing how close we had come to losing him as well. How had I missed the impact Miley's passing would have on him? And why did I think it was the right time to bring up past behaviors?

Looking back, it's still painful to see that we tried to address his behavioral issues at such a raw time. Reading the transcript for the first time, I felt horrified by my own insensitivity. I just wanted to pick him up, hold him, and apologize for being thoughtless during his time of grief. At the time, we had no idea the depth of communication that would be possible, and we approached that first session as if it might be our only opportunity with him. It never occurred to us that Sprout would be grieving Miley as deeply as we were, and that there was no space for old wounds. I still ask myself, *How could I have been so heartless?*

The session revealed so much about Sprout's past and his loving, resilient spirit. Since that day, we've never used the words "bad dog" around him, making sure instead to tell him daily what a "good dog" he is. With Miley gone, we decided he should never be left home alone if we could help it, and if he had to be with others or come as a guest, we hoped to help him be more comfortable in different settings. But knowing the trauma he'd endured broke my heart, and since then, helping him heal has been our mission.

Learning that losing Miley had temporarily jolted Sprout out of his body brought back a memory. When I was a teenager, my grandmother passed away unexpectedly after a routine surgery. My grandfather was devastated, and my parents were so grateful he had the comfort of their little dog, Mia. But that very night, Mia also passed away—she seemed like a healthy, middle-aged dog with no medical issues. For years, my dad was angry about Mia's passing. Now, I wonder if Mia was jolted out of her body just as Sprout nearly was, except she had no one to guide her back. Looking back, I can't imagine what it would have been like to lose Sprout right after Miley, and I am forever indebted to Elizabeth for bringing him back to us

Sprout's relationship with my mother changed when she developed Alzheimer's. He'd always liked her, but once her dementia set in, he devoted himself to her with a remarkable attentiveness. Whenever we visited, he'd ignore everyone else and go straight to her, curling up in her lap, giving her his undivided attention and devotion.

She'd calm visibly when he was with her, and his presence seemed to ease her confusion and anxiety. It was unexpectedly beautiful to witness his innate ability to comfort her, and I will always be grateful to him for this.

Was this really Miley and Sprout? We didn't ask Elizabeth for "proof" or pose any trick questions. We went into that first session with open hearts, willing to trust the process until something told us otherwise. Years later, I still trust this process without question. Miley and Sprout's personalities came through so vividly that each interaction felt undeniably real with each of their unique personalities shining through.

In Miley's session, she said, "I am an excellent Commander, and yes, I was in my joy with many to command, who all loved me, and respected me, even more." That was Miley to the core. Beneath her cute, fluffy exterior, she was a true Commander. And though we all knew this side of her, Elizabeth didn't—she couldn't have known how fitting this statement was.

In Sprout's session, when Elizabeth started touching on topics that made him anxious, she described him as "shifting his weight back and forth from left to right." This is something Sprout always does when he's stressed—a behavior so frequent that we'd even given it a nickname, "the little match girl dance." Elizabeth had no way of knowing this. Both Miley and Sprout's personalities came through so clearly, but these small details truly validated that Elizabeth was communicating with them directly. Since that first session, there have been many moments like this—little quirks Elizabeth couldn't have known—that continually assure us of their presence.

After those first eye-opening sessions, our whole perspective shifted. The transcripts were a shock, revealing a depth and complexity we hadn't expected. Moving forward, we began crafting questions differently, seeking not only to understand but to engage with these multidimensional beings.

Of course, we scheduled a second session for each of them. That first session had helped us navigate Miley's passing and gave us insight into Sprout's unique history. But we'd opened Pandora's box, glimpsing a world that we had somehow missed until now. Our initial questions brought some answers but also left us with countless new questions.

I found myself wondering, *"What should I ask next?"* On one hand, I was curious about the limits of Miley's abilities and what she might be willing to share. But part of me simply wanted to reconnect with them—to know what they were doing, thinking, and feeling. It felt like having a window into a world I'd thought was beyond reach, one that brought me closer to the ones I loved.

While we were navigating the world of spirit connections, the physical world demanded our attention in equally complex ways. My mother's dementia was advancing, like a slow-moving train I couldn't stop, just watching as it approached a tragic derailment. Our business was at its peak, but we had it up for sale, hoping to reclaim our lives. I wanted to spend more time with my parents, while Dene wanted to be there for his father, who had been diagnosed with Lewy-Body dementia in California. We had recently purchased an Airstream trailer, intending of being able to travel between California and Massachusetts, but selling the business was key to freeing up that time. Until then, the Airstream sat waiting in the driveway, a symbol of the life we were working toward.

CHAPTER SEVEN

January 11: Excerpts From Miley's 2nd Session

*N*ote to Reader: I've come to realize there's no end to what I want to understand about Miley, Sprout, all animals, and life's mysteries. I could spend every day exploring these questions and still find new avenues to uncover. While I've gathered years of conversations with Miley, Sprout, Keisha, and others, from this point on, I've chosen to share selected excerpts from our sessions, focusing on the themes most relevant to this journey of healing, loss, and transformation. These passages capture essential moments and insights without the complete transcripts, which have covered a wide range of topics. The intention is to provide a focused narrative, staying within the scope of this bo ok.

Email arrives from Elizabeth:

Hi Lisa and Dene,

Miley had a whole download waiting for us. She is pretty organized, which is very helpful. Part of that is due to your own effort in preparing the questions, as she starts the session then on her end.

Miley has known what she wants to teach you from the outset. She's probably been forming this for years.

Elizabeth

Session starts:

Miley sends as I look at her picture and close my eyes to connect: I am so much bigger than that. She shows me where you are on your path, there is as much to unlearn, as there is to learn, and that the unlearning, the discarding of the energy, beliefs and emotions that you hold that is not yours; is a necessary first step. This is to free your energy field, mental/emotional body, and even physical body of that clutter so that you can open up to more of who you really are. She shows me a tight bud at your core, unfolding as you release what you are not.

E: Thank you, Miley; that is a wonderful way to start today.

M: You see, when you incarnate into this Earth realm, there are many rules and conditions for each stage of experiencing a life on Earth. We do not mean life stage, we are talking about stages of spiritual development. Some call these dimensional experiences or other evolutional references. It is quite complex. I am with some of your guides who desire to help you understand, in a simple big picture way, what you are embarking upon.

E: Miley, please continue.

M: Thank you (she graciously accepts the floor, which she had already taken, I am laughing). So you have arrived on Earth, and you have no remembrance of who you really are, where you come from, how you got here, what your plans were, your purpose, or where you will go next. But, you have your heart, and that is your true guiding system. You also have many clues and past relics of those who have gone before you, traveling to this planet as various species, for a large variety of purposes. Not all who have come to Earth have been upon the path of discovery and remembering the truth and the power of the spark of the divine within. So there currently are and have been other travelers as well.

There are many, many guidebooks written. Most all were written in the context of their time epoch, many with true spiritual input, much of that eroded or out of context over time. Your guidebook is written in your heart, and you will discover it as you unlearn all that others have thought it best, or, well, perhaps even profitable, for you to learn. There are many games within the main game, upon Earth.

So we suggest two places for you to start: One is your heart. Dene, you in particular have less distractions in getting to that doorway. You are both so beautiful, in your hearts, and so different, in your makeup. This is a place you want to move into and use as your guidance system. For now, we suggest you keep an image of your heartspace as a navigational tool, in your intentions. Get comfortable with it and learn to recognize when you are in that space, vs when you are in your mental space. What is the difference between the two. You know you can think with your heart. Intend to notice where you are thinking from.

Two: Use the process of sorting. Allow what you are not to fall away. As you realize these thoughts, feelings, beliefs, dreams and realities that were pressed upon you as not yours, let them release. These are the ones you absorbed, picked up, accepted in varying degrees of enthusiasm or even those that you reluctantly merged with. Then, intentionally ask to know more of what you are, to fill in the space. Ask to stumble upon pieces of the perspectives that will show you the closest truths that you can absorb from your current frequency.

You see, as you become more of your True Self, your frequency will rise, and like climbing a mountain, you will be able to see from a higher perspective. It is that simple, for now.

You want to know the greatest truths, in great detail, especially you, Lisa.

I would give you these truths, as I access them through your own trusty guides, yet you would not hear them well right now. What I will give you instead, are the steps slightly ahead of you.

Accept the present moment as your teaching spot. Just sit down in it. Be. Learn to go inward first. You can interpret that as a way to start your day, or you can take that into moments of your day where you have an urge to figure something out, to know more. Set your energy, and then intention. Do not set your energy as 'tired, grumpy or worried'. Answers that match those frequencies will not help you. Choose where you want to start your energy. I suggest peace, or happy, or content, if you do not know where you want to set your energy. Then, ask for what you need to know right now, continuing to feel those emotions. Stay connected to your heart, stay peaceful. Hold that vibration as you begin to move, go outward, go about your day. Keep it simple and you will know what you need.

This is a process you can always use. You can expand it, hone it, transform it, embellish it; but the basic process that will take you where you want to go is within this structure. Your task is to learn to release what's not you and in the way, as you embrace what and who you are, and bring what you want to know to you. You are not Tired, Grumpy or Worried. You may feel that way, but it is more a habit, that you perhaps learned from someone else, than your own innate frequency

E: Thank you, Miley. I was completely unprepared for you to download all this initially. Lisa and Dene have carefully prepared and revised their questions for you today.

M: (Sends me a raised eyebrow energy) Oh? And you think that was simply Lisa and Dene?

E: (Laughing) No, I think you were with them, of course, Miley.

M: (Moves out of the humor) The part of this communication where Lisa and Dene form their questions is very important. For clarity, you could not 'skip' that part, and simply say, Miley tell us what we need to know. You see, when you sit to write, or pause to think, your own guides notice. Who are you thinking about? Oh, Miley. Your guides immediately move into 'We'll have our people reach out to your people' mode, sending an energetic conduit, to me through my own guides, so that there is an overall dynamic forming that includes and connects you, your guides, me, my own guides, the scribe (that's me, Elizabeth), her guides, her library and all of our libraries, into a matrix.

We are all participants, benefitting and learning from this process. You may think this is about your own spiritual growth, Lisa and Dene; but it is also a process of sharing and exchanging that enriches all who participate or experience this, even those 'bystanders' that you choose to share the recorded version of this interchange with. Why do you think your guides are so eager to help? It is because their purpose is to assist you, guide you, but they benefit from this process as much as you do. Does this help you see more of the true balance of the nature of the Universe, simply within our very small process?

E: That is a really helpful perspective, Miley, and somehow imbues a certain gratitude for the divine operating systems that are always functioning, if we look for them. Maybe it somewhat relates to what people mean when they speak in terms of Divine Providence?

M: In the sense that all are affected by all, in the upward spiral format of growth, yes. In the downward spiral of dropping resonance, yes too, but few are interested in hearing or learning more about that.

E: Right. Miley, are you at a point where you would like to fill in some details and hear the questions from Lisa, Dene and your own energetic input? The collaborative questions?

M: Yes, we have downloaded the main structure of what we wish to offer you as focus today. Lisa and Dene, you want to know everything now. You will know everything you want to know, but only if you absorb it in a manner that is realistic for your human earth frequency positions. Dene, you become intoxicated with the truth. This is not a bad thing at all, it is simply to recognize your thirst. Your heart and soul are pulling you hard forward. Spend extra time in FOCUSED, aware meditation in order to lay in the structure of understanding as you move forward. Ground regularly, and connect the architecture of what you know, that is yours, with your heart knowledge. Your knowingness is valuable; do not throw that baby out with the bathwater. You surrender easily. Be aware of that skill, and stay in balance. Stay present, even as your heart soars and your Soul pulls you.

Lisa, your point of balance is almost the reverse, in some ways. You must learn to step out of your vast body of accumulated knowledge. The best stuff will come when the need of your mind to know or control; is balanced with your ability to surrender to the process of simply opening your heart, and staying in the present moment, experiencing the energy of the divine. There is your carrot on the stick: Your most valuable stored knowledge will be accessible to you then. What you have now (in terms of knowledge) is cotton candy.

E: Miley, the way you talk so candidly to Lisa and Dene is full of love. And terribly funny to me. I'm going to start, from Lisa and Dene:

"Dene and I love you with all of our hearts and want to tell you how grateful we are to have you in our lives and have this opportunity to take our relationship to another level. It is our goal to develop open and regular communication with you, if that is something that you also would like to pursue. We are intending to take the animal communication classes with Elizabeth in order to learn how to develop our communication abilities, but also would like to have instruction from you on what other things we can do."

M: Dear Lisa (very softly), the best overall channel is through your heart, as described. If you will pay attention to the main suggestions I have made you will start to notice more. I say that because as you clearly understand, that is what needs to happen to fulfill your desire: I, and all of your guides, send regular communication and signs. We also observe and note what you are able to receive and works for you. The adjustments are mostly on this end. However, when you make the suggested adjustments - and they are large format suggestions, not detailed because you are not in a space yet where details will assist you; we will notice and flow more to you in the spaces where you best receive. So rather than going outside of yourself looking, work on receiving. You will learn a lot about the receiving place in the animal communication classes.

Animals are always communicating; it is when humans learn to receive that they recognize that. There is a lot of competition for your receptors on Earth - look at the explosion of information. All of it competes for attention - your attention. What good is a social media post if no one sees it? So if you get bored and want to work on 'extra credit', notice your receptors - notice when, how and where you receive information, on a daily basis. You might want to consciously become more in charge of selecting which receptors to turn on and off. E: Ha - you're at the next part of the question, Miley. "While we are learning to "listen" better, we were thinking that maybe there could be some ways we could know that you are sending us a message."

M: At first, we will mostly communicate inwardly, through the heart, through your dreams, but yes Lisa we also do communicate in many ways, wondering what you will receive.

(To you both) The answer to all of your 'Was that you, Miley?' questions is Yes. That you thought of that experience as you wrote the question, is your answer. Yes, that was me. And, I am always thrilled when you recognize me, even if you need validation. Who else would it be? Right now? I have your attention, as your guides can attest to by their swarming actions. (some humor inflection)

E: Dene and Lisa ask: "Are there any colors or numbers that we should associate with you? Any that we could associate with yes/no answers?"

M: These are the wanting to know, and the wanting to know details origination questions, Lisa. They are not bad questions, they are actually good questions, but it is like you have brought two stacks of library books to the desk to check out, each stack towering over your head, having to make two trips, the books falling over, and the librarian looking at you, wondering how you can possibly get through all these books in two weeks. (she runs me through those images). There is excellent information for you in all the books, but we must start with the foundation, as outlined.

And I will not forget your requests. I will show you, as we discover them on our journey.

E: Miley, I thank you so much for all that you are giving to all of us. Lisa and Dene have more questions for another time.

M: There is no loss in revising the questions again and again. It is actually a process of gain, of knowing. You will come upon your own answers to much between now and then.

E:. Bye, for now.

Session ends.

Elizabeth

LISA'S REACTION:

Seeing how prepared Miley was, with so much material ready to share, made me realize just how true Elizabeth's words were—Miley has been waiting for this. She has a vast amount of wisdom to impart, and she's going to share it regardless of what questions we might ask. At some point, we just accept this; after all, she is The Commander.

In Miley's big "download," she advises us to set our energy and intention for the day. This advice has been transformative for Dene and me. We now start each day by telling each other, "Good morning! It's going to be a GREAT day!"—and, magically, it is a great day. This simple but powerful practice has taught us that happiness is a choice and that by setting an intention, we are choosing in advance how we'll experience the day. This intention aligns our energy and focus toward positivity, almost like setting a course on a map. So even if challenges arise, we're primed to respond with an openness to see the good. Thank you, Miley; that was a big one!

Each time I revisit these sessions, I see something new that surprises me. Miley said: *"You may think this is about your own spiritual growth, Lisa and Dene; but it is also a process of sharing and exchanging that enriches all who participate or experience this, even those 'bystanders' that you choose to share the recorded version of this interchange with."*

At the time, I thought Miley was referring to the fact that I had shared the first session with my brother. But in later sessions, she alludes more than once to what we will accomplish together, and now here we are, sharing her words in this book, opening possibilities for whatever we may create next.

It also amuses me how Miley describes the way Dene and I each search for knowledge and truth. She first describes Dene and then adds, *"Lisa, your point of balance is almost the reverse."* I find this hilarious because Dene and I are SO very different. Elizabeth had only interacted with us twice and still hardly knew us, but anyone who does would likely agree that Miley's observation is spot on. I sometimes think Dene and I succeed in so many of our endeavors precisely because we are opposites, nearly always approaching things from completely different directions. It brings me a lot of joy to see Miley noticing—and commenting on—that dynamic more than once.

CHAPTER EIGHT

January 11: Excerpts from Sprout's 2nd Session

Email arrives from Elizabeth:

Sprout is doing so well! He is sturdy, soft, happy, maybe still a little tentative in ways but he has a role in this too. Twice he brought up 'rushing' or being rushed, so my only comment is to let him know that if you need to rush out the door, or do something quickly, or you feel rushed - it has nothing to do with him, and he can take his time. Sprout has some real wisdom to offer, and he let us know he will continue to grow into more of that.

Elizabeth

Session starts:

Sprout says to me: I'm here.

E: Hi Sprout! Welcome! I see you are bringing in so much more of your ethereal influences - I don't remember seeing so much Fae energy around you last time.

S: I'm doing what they are supposed to do (you two). That's my new job now. I'm boots on the ground. But I'm softer inside too, so you may have to listen harder to me. Exercise your ears. I'm really happy now. Miley is where she should be - in the air, not here thumping the Earth. Her energy was always so loud - I had to close my ears.

E: That's very interesting, Sprout. Congratulations on your progress - you seem to be doing so well. Lisa and Dene have a message for you: "We love you so very much and want you to know you ARE A GOOD DOG/BE-ING. You are safe and loved with us and we hope that you feel that. Is there anything we can do to help you feel that?"

S: I'm feeling into that. (He shows me a picture of his energy beginning to fill up his big tall 'boots on the ground') I'm taking my time because that's what it takes.

E: And that is excellent Sprout - no one is rushing you.

S: Then who are they rushing?

E: I think that might be just excitement you're showing me?

S: I feel pressure but I don't think it's for me.

E: I don't think so either, so don't worry about it. We humans do that to ourselves sometimes when playing games with ourselves. I find myself playing that game too. Please ignore human behavior when you know it's not about you.

S: Ok. I can do that.

E: Lisa and Dene also ask you: "Is there anything you would like to tell us about your mission or contracts?"

S: (Very happily) I just announced my new one! Follow me. I'm the Follow me truck (he shows me the little trucks that used to drive back and forth around construction site on highways when one lane is closed, having the line of waiting cars follow it safely around the construction)

E: That's kind of an old fashioned symbol, Sprout - is there any reason you picked that to show me?

S: I'm like the little truck that shows the 18 wheelers where to go. It doesn't matter that I'm small; I can pace you. I'm not rushing, you noticed?

E: That's true - you did show us that right off. That's extremely helpful, and you are contributing greatly to Dene and Lisa's spiritual quest. Also, you are right there with them, to show them, in the physical. This is wonderful, Sprout.

S: Boots on the ground!

E: Your heart feels so happy.

S: I like my new job.

E: Lisa and Dene - (Sprout interrupts me)

S: It's as important as Miley's.

E: Yes! It is. All that info is dependent on Lisa and Dene using it, following it, in their daily lives, in order to be fruitful. Thank you for your part, again.

S: Ok. I just wanted to make sure you all realized that. Go on.

E: Thank you! Continuing: "When you first came to us they said your name was Napoleon. We did not feel that was right and thought Sprout was a better fit. Are you happy with this name or do you think of yourself with another name?"

S: I think Sprout grows better than Napoleon, don't you?

E: I do. You like your name signifying growth?

S: Well that's what I'm showing the way for, isn't it?

E: It is. It's perfect, then. Thank you for keeping it simple.

S: See, I am VERY good at that, and that is what is most needed for balance with all you eager lofty Beings. (he looks around) Our home is full of interested parties.

E: Do you have a light/dark frequency meter available when you observe these parties, Sprout?

S: Yes I do. I have a zapper handy too if they're not light. (he shows me he has a guide who removes negative presences.)

E: You are armed and able!

S: I have everything I need to do my job. (To you all) You do too.

E: Dene and Lisa ask: "Is there anything you would like to share about how you are feeling or what you need?"

S: I think I shared it. I think now that Dene and Lisa have been advised, all will go well. I'd like a little extra cuddle time. I'm cuddlier now, and sometimes I need a little encouragement to be ok with that.

E: Oh, ok sure - I'm sure you will have that, then. Thank you for pointing that out.

S: Mostly I'm fine. Happy.

E: Dene and Lisa ask: "Are there any colors or numbers that we can associate with you?"

S: I'm always partial to green, since I'm aligned with growth. Frogs are my friends, as they are symbols of growth. It is true that I have been able to connect with the Fairie realm more, now that Miley is not scaring them off.

E: Hm, did you feel she did that intentionally, Sprout?

S: Oh no. It's just they are refined energy. I think Miley's energy was made of bricks.

E: Miley is/was a powerful Being in her own realm.

S: She's happier now too, I think. She couldn't boss everyone around quite as much as she wanted to when she was stuck in a dog body.

E: Good point, although she obviously loved it too.

S: She did. Miley is my friend but we are very different.

E: Do you feel stuck in a dog body?

S: Oh no my body is perfect now. I just needed more space, and now I have it. (He shows me frequency as space - Miley's tended to override his own, which is in a way higher, lighter, in the body)

E: From Lisa and Dene: "We want you to know that you provide us both with so much comfort and joy. We are both very grateful that you are spending this incarnation with us."

S: Me too. You'll be even more grateful later because I am an excellent Being of Service, and my old contracts were muddy, torn and unclear. I didn't know what to do. Now I do.

E: That's wonderful, Sprout. We're all happy that you are benefitting from assisting as well. This is truly a collaborative experience.

S: I am wiser than you know. Watch me grow.

E: (Me, laughing with tears) I can't wait, Sprout. Is there anything else you'd like to say or ask?

S: Nope, I said good words. I'm done. Thank you. Bye!

Session ends.

Elizabeth

LISA'S REACTION:

It was such a relief to hear what Sprout had to say this time. He's clearly found a new purpose and seems more relaxed, which is a comfort to us. We love that he's taken on the role of "boots on the ground"—it's such a fitting description for him and the current situation. This session raised a whole new set of questions, as we're beginning to see there's much more to Sprout than we had ever realized. He's changing, coming into his own with a newfound confidence and happiness. It's not that he's happier because Miley is gone, but because we're finally addressing his own needs, growth, and purpose. He's really stepped up.

We can see how well he's adjusting to our little family of three. We decided to leave Miley's beds around, and interestingly, Sprout began using them all the time. Previously, he never went near her beds, but now he's taken them over, even though they're hilariously oversized for him.

His comments about the Fae realm were unexpected but explained some odd occurrences over the years in our home. Mostly, though, it's heartwarming to see Sprout happy and embracing this new normal.

All that being said - it's clear how deeply Sprout is affected by the changes around him. His emotional responses—grief, confusion, and a need for reassurance—are reminders that our animals are not simply "along for the ride" but are deeply entwined with our lives, experiencing their own powerful feelings and interpretations. This session with Sprout opened my eyes to the responsibility we have in honoring our pets' emotional lives, especially during times of transition. It's a lesson I now carry forward: to consciously check in with Sprout and to recognize him as a sensitive, aware being who benefits from our understanding and support, just as much as any human family member would.

We're getting a handle on who Miley and Sprout really are, recognizing that they have access to knowledge beyond our own. Sprout has taken on the role of grounding us in the present, offering his steady guidance and gentle humor to help us navigate life's complexities. Miley, however, exists on a different plane entirely—one where time and space dissolve, and her insights reach far beyond the everyday. With her guidance, I realized I could ask questions about some of the most complex challenges we face, including my mother's Alzheimer's and how to support my father as her caregiver. The profound wisdom they both bring is a reminder that love, whether in the form of grounding support or spiritual guidance, transcends all boundaries.

CHAPTER NINE

January 21: Excerpts From Miley's 3rd Session

Email arrives from Elizabeth:

Miley has moved into a more defined role as teacher and guide, and she uses every question to teach. Her organization is even more immaculate than last time. She is training you to learn as students, and offered very helpful advice in terms of the questions you asked.

Elizabeth

Session starts:

As I begin to focus on Miley, she shows me that she is an expert in guidance on emotional attunement, meaning understanding of emotions, and adjustments that can be made for balance and wholeness. She also shows me that general knowledge regarding the role of judgements within the human condition, third dimension; is closely allied with this type of expertise. She is showing me herself as stepping into a more specific role as guide.

This is part of her process of finding her place where she is now.

Note: When I use 'we' instead of 'I', in referring to her, it is because your guides have joined her in the specific message.

Miley...?

M: Yes. Present.

E: You are more serious today.

M: It is a serious conversation. (She shows me she has heard your pleas for her assistance). Yet, perhaps the situation is not as fraught with the sense of dire straits, as my dear humans may be experiencing it. May I explain?

E: Sure. (I have no idea where she is going with this)

M: You see, Lisa, you especially, but you too at times, Dene; you have spent a better portion of a lifetime moving in and out of emotional overwhelm, as a navigational tool. Imagine that you are sailing, in a boat. You have calm waters, you have a steady wind, the sun is shining. You love life, you truly do. Yet when the skies darken, the wind picks up, changing direction suddenly; the waves increase and the ride becomes choppy.

How do you respond?

And how do you choose to respond?

Do you, CHOOSE to respond?

Or do you react?

This is what I feel is most important to address within the context of the requests today. This is where the root cause of your distress lies. Understanding that can help you navigate with less distress. That is my purpose, in assisting you: To help you grow, navigate life more smoothly, so that MORE of your time is spent enjoying the ride, regardless of the water conditions.

E: I see, Miley. I do have questions and messages for you. Would you like to say more about this now, or should I start with the questions.

M: Let us proceed. What do my dear humans present? (She is flowing more nurturing and love towards you two now, and towards the extended family, as if she was a wise governess. She seems more sure-footed in her definition of how she can best assist this time)

E: From Lisa:"Duke (my dad) and Grandma (my mom) both of whom you know very well, have events unfolding that I am trying to make the best decisions I can for both of them."

M: Yes, you are. Simply put, Lisa, if you would lean a little less, and spend a little more time in your heart center, quiet, still, it would be most beneficial. We understand the challenge, however. The waves are 25 feet tall, right now, approaching your boat.

E: "I feel like my mom only has "one toe left in her physical body" now, kind of like you said about yourself when you still had a body with us. Do you agree with that and do you think there is anything more we can be doing to help her and Duke right now that we aren't doing?"

M: It is a far more complex situation than the analogy I used to show you where I was on my journey. Should I explain?

E: I think this is what they really want assistance with, so yes, Miley, please.

M: Humans, upon incarnating into the Earth plane, cannot carry all of their light with them, as they descend into the density of the 3rd dimension. This is changing, but our beloved Grandma and Duke entered the 3rd dimension when they incarnated, as you did, so we will start here.

Imagine, as an analogy, that you are ascending a very high mountain. As the elevation increases, there is less oxygen available, you grow more tired, you leave items behind in order to acclimate to the new environment. The same process occurs with humans as they descend through the dimensional layers, down into the 3rd dimension. You cannot fit all of your light into this body. So what do you do, with the parts of you that don't fit? There is the complicating piece that you are a perfect Being, and Earth is an imperfect place, so you cannot incarnate with perfection. The very short answer is you split yourself into 11 experiences, simultaneously. You might call these other dimensional experiences, or parallel lives. All must enter the Earth plane simultaneously in order for this process to work, and all must exit at the exact same time in order to reunite into wholeness, as well. The 11 selves have similar lives, yet expressing different parts of your perfection. Are you really bad at sports? One of your dimensional selves is an expert ice skater, a champion, etc. I am keeping this very basic, for the purpose of you understanding that as your mother prepares to depart, she must align with the other of her

Selves who are experiencing their own versions of life, in order to exit. She is ready, maybe some others are too; but others are not, yet. Have you ever tried to get 11 people together for a meeting or an event? This is your mother's primary focus right now.

What is very convenient, and of great assistance in this process now, is finding a way to 'wait', after you are complete. Your mother is complete, and needs to wait until the other versions of her Self are complete. A long illness, particularly dementia, is very helpful as it fulfills the technical requirements of timing, yet allows most of her spirit to begin to explore other realms and look at the path ahead, almost as a 'scout' for her Perfected Self, when all unite and proceed.

What you and Duke can do to assist her most right now, is to align with her process, pull your own energies back, and allow her to do what she needs to do. Of course, within social contexts and with your love and desire to avoid trauma for her, you need to keep the body safe. You can also keep the mental and emotional body safe, by coming into a state of peace, love and allowance. Keep your own judgments, beliefs, emotions and any stressors, outside of her energy field. This is of great assistance in allowing her to let go, to move through her process, unfettered by concerns about the loved ones she is leaving behind.

Most humans are not aware of this process, and in their group beliefs, run many actions and emotions that counter the process and make it more difficult for the one who is crossing. We take the time to explain this because we believe it will be of the most assistance that we can give in helping you manage your emotions and actions in order to truly assist your mother.

E: Thank you Miley. From Lisa: "Because of her Alzheimer's, Mom went into the hospital today with a urinary tract infection and when she comes back we have to move her out of her apartment with Duke in assisted living, and into the memory care wing without him. We need to move her into a unit with a roommate and I'm not sure if that is the right decision."

M: Dear Lisa, it does not really matter, at this point, especially if you relax your concern about this choice, roommate or no, and remove your attention point from that choice, and release any impending judgment regarding did we do the right thing?

E: From Lisa:"I am worried about her and also about Duke feeling guilty about moving her, and her adjusting, and would like to hear your thoughts/advice."

M: "I am worried." Please, Lisa, notice this. The easiest solution is to not worry.

To assist, as you can, bring your mother's process to Duke's attention, and how to allow her to release as described. And if you can, suggest to Duke that guilt is a most useless emotion: It offers no assistance or benefit to anyone involved. You will know if you can share this perspective with him. I will assist you in that I can intervene gently, and attempt to help by providing openings in conversations with him. Just call me in, and relax, take all of your energy out of his space. What that looks like is you are with him, quietly, calmly, centered in your heart, and neutral. Allow him to begin to present his thoughts, and if you can, move towards sharing feelings in your conversation. That is the point where I will attempt to assist with an opening for sharing, in the way that he can absorb the information. We may be successful in our joint venture, but he may not be ready for this type of considering at this time.

E: Thank you, Miley. Do you want to say anything else about that?

M: We are complete in these questions.

LISA'S REACTION:

Miley's lessons here have been invaluable, and there are so many. Her analogy of the boat as part of the lesson to respond instead of react was incredibly helpful. I have spent so much of my life reacting, but now I choose to respond. My life is better for it. Sometimes I forget and react, but in general, this is a lesson I've embraced.

I learned that when an "event" happens, our immediate reaction is often a flood of hormones—fear, anger, or joy—and after a few minutes, those hormones dissipate. What happens after that is our choice: we can choose our response. This realization was so freeing. When something distressing happens, I take a deep breath, let the initial reaction settle, and then respond. It's not always perfect, but it's a vastly different path. I rarely indulge in emotions like fear or anger now; if I catch myself, I try to redirect and choose a different response. The more I practice this, the more natural it becomes.

In managing my parents' transition, Miley's wisdom was especially helpful. Mom had been struggling with Alzheimer's, and Dad was her main caregiver. Making the decision to move them into assisted living was incredibly hard. Dad was in good health and didn't need assistance, but Mom's condition was progressing. I had asked Dad to let me know when he felt he couldn't manage, but as I saw him becoming worn down, I realized he'd never admit it. So, my brother and I stepped in and made the difficult decision.

Moving them to assisted living was painful, especially with the pandemic restrictions. We weren't allowed to help them move in; we unloaded their belongings on the sidewalk, handed them over to staff, and didn't know when we'd see them face to face again, if ever. When it was time to move Mom to memory care, Miley's advice about her transition process gave me peace and the strength to make these hard decisions. It allowed me to spend my remaining time with her in peace, so I wouldn't bring pain or stress into her space when I visited. This was an incredible gift.

To this day, I feel that losing Miley, then having these sessions, prepared me for the eventual loss of my mother. When that day came, I was able to accept it in a way I wouldn't have been able to before.

On a lighter note, Dene and I took an animal communication class with Elizabeth. Dene was excellent at it, while I...struggled. As Dene would be the first to tell you, I am not a great listener, which I am working on! I did learn something priceless, though: if you feel your animal is telling you something, they are. It's not imagination; we really do pick up on their "transmissions." This awareness has deepened my connection with Sprout, and I now recognize a lot more of what he's trying to communicate.

Sometimes, his "transmissions" are so obvious that it's laughable—especially when treats are involved. Sprout gets his treats at the same time every afternoon, and he absolutely knows what time it is. Before he goes to great lengths to get my attention and dramatically draw my gaze to the treat jar, I can feel him telling me: *It's time.* It's as if he's saying, *Don't forget—I'm watching the clock for you!*

The more we recognize that these thoughts originated from our animals and not ourselves, the better we are at "hearing" them. To quote Sprout: "It's not so complicated."

CHAPTER TEN

Summer Sessions Excerpts - With Miley

JULY 6TH

E: From Lisa: "When you are in an animal body, are there two "yous" that I am interacting with simultaneously? For instance, is Miley the dog more interested in treats and sniffing things, and Miley my guide/teacher/nurturer your higher self present, but not necessarily the one responding to my interactions on the physical level? And will it be different next time you come back?" Miley, I am breaking these questions up into parts in hopes that it is easier for you to address them.

M: There are multiple 'mes'. A body is an access point, and sharing is common in the animal kingdom. We can see and experience perspectives beyond the veil, which is where your questions are directed: Miley, tell me about what I can't see. Of course we wish to teach you to see, because we do not know exactly what you see and what you don't see. That is why we drive the bus as we do. I am consciously multidimensional. You are unconsciously multidimensional but becoming more conscious. You (she directs this to me) sometimes delineates this with addressing us as "Miley the Earthdog", and just "Miley".

E: I do, especially when there are questions about the body, eating habits, etc.

M: It is extremely fluid, Lisa, far more than you can imagine. That is the experience you will have when you return Home, to the other side of the veil after your visit to Earth. You will have many pictures to show and stories to tell. You will remember them all, the instant your energy goes to them. This is similar to how I experience Earth, and how most animals experience multidimensionality within the context of interacting with unconscious humans. What is the easiest way to do that? Teach the humans to become conscious! (She looks at me.)

E: Yes, got it Miley, that's our service, here. (From Lisa still) What about next time you come back?

M: I will be wildly different, yet you will recognize me as Miley. My intention would never be to repeat a life, and you would never have that intention either. I am excited and await my next adventure, know this.

E: From Lisa: "Next time will Miley the physical be more "aware" or was Miley the physical always "aware" and it was just us that was not aware? How does that work?"

M: You will understand this better through observation than in any way that I could explain in words to you. The reason is that your brain is not yet optimized to understand this. As you work with, talk to, and experience connections with animals and your heart, grow your own spirituality, your own brain restructures. That is the process of remembering. This is how it works. Do you see this? I can endeavor to 'show' you as you experience life, yet if I tell you, you will not get very much of it, and possibly make false assumptions based on the gaps in what you do get. Aha moments are much fuller and more accurate, and anchor the realizations more deeply.

LISA'S THOUGHTS

Reflecting here, I find myself circling back to an ongoing question: if animals are indeed complex, multidimensional beings, then why can't I seem to communicate with Sprout on that same level? How much does he understand when I talk to him? This theme keeps resurfacing for me, and while Miley's answers offer new perspectives, my curiosity remains.

Miley's wisdom was profound, helping me see how we and our animals exist on multiple levels of awareness. Her guidance encouraged me to let go of the need to know exactly what my animals understand and instead focus on observing and trusting their wisdom in ways I couldn't before.

With everything else going on in my life, this has all been a lot to absorb. Luckily, Miley is a patient Being who loves me, even when I would sidetrack from my "lessons" to ask things like, "Is Bigfoot real?" and "Is there really a Loch Ness Monster?" (Yes to both of those, in case you're wondering!)

Sometimes I just needed to lean on Miley in unexpected ways and lighten things up, because some hard moments were coming.

AUGUST 3RD

E: From Lisa: "I feel like my mom is going to die/transition right in the middle of all of this (the sale of our business was in its final weeks.) Can you tell me if I am right? And what is the reason that this is all happening at the same time? Is it a test?"

M: It is not a test, it is a complicated run to the county dump. We do not disparage any of this, least of all your dear mother's crossing. There is no set timing on her exit plan; she has optional times of crossing - multiple ones, as you all do. You all have many exit doors, and you choose one, according to how things are as you approach your exit plan epoch in life. Some take decades, some take 10 minutes when the first crossing opportunity is approached. It is up to her, and it is about her, and your most helpful role is to let go, and allow her to proceed upon her own timeline. (She softens, leans in.) Try to move out of a thought process of are you right or wrong in guessing when she will leave. It is a slow transition, as you are observing - 40-50% of her is already out of the body. Sometimes these slow transitions last a long time because the person is having a hard time getting that last 3% out: Letting go. You can help her by letting go on your end. Now, sometimes long goodbyes have a purpose, but mostly it is simply entanglement, and more difficult than not for all concerned. If you can stand at a distance, observe FROM YOUR HEART, know that all is well in the Universe; this is a sacred process and you ARE correct that she will be joyously welcomed home, this will be the highest act of service that you can perform for your mother, and your Self. This is a 5D place to witness her crossing from. She is graduating, with honors. You will too, when you move out of your body, but that is a long way off, Lisa, so focus on what life without encumbrances really means for you: What will you Choose? We know you are entwined with your mother. Try to disentangle. Review from the Heart. (She is sending you much love and support, here.)

LISA'S REACTION:

In these excerpts, I feel Miley is offering both practical guidance and profound lessons in trust, letting go, and honoring each being's individual timeline and journey. Her way of explaining my mom's "long goodbye" as a sacred, personal process—one filled with choices—has been especially grounding, and also freeing in a way. Miley's encouragement to witness from a place of love and peace has strengthened me during the difficult decisions about my mom's care.

These sessions have deepened my respect for my animals—all animals—as wise, loving beings with their own profound insights. I am only beginning to understand the depth of their wisdom and the incredible journey we are on together.

Through Miley's lessons, I'm learning to release the need to control or predict the timing of events, especially when it came to my mother's passing. Miley reminded me that this sacred transition was ultimately my mother's journey, and the most loving thing I could do was witness it with peace and acceptance.

Letting go of control hasn't always been easy for me. I naturally want to understand, to plan, and to know what's coming—especially regarding my connection with my mother, or Miley. But Miley's guidance here has encouraged me to step back, release my grip, and let life flow more freely. Trusting that the right insights and outcomes will come in their own time, I've found a new sense of peace and openness along this journey.

MOM

On September 14th, 2021, my mom crossed over. She was 83 years old. We had known we were getting close to the end, and that morning I was already on my way to see her when the hospice nurse called to say she thought Mom was starting to transition. My brother and my dad met me there at her bedside. The three of us sat with her for hours, and although she was not conscious, I felt she knew we were there, holding her hand. I knew Miley was there with us also, and that gave me comfort and strength. In the final moment, Mom's eyes fluttered open briefly. Dad leaned over, gave her a kiss, and then she just slipped away.

It's been just over three years since that moment, and it still makes me cry. I miss her terribly. We had some rough times when I was a teenager, but we grew close in the decades that followed. Losing Miley first had prepared me for this in ways I could never have predicted. I immediately felt the pain of losing Mom, but now I knew she wasn't truly gone, and I knew she was not far, and that she could hear me. I told her that my brother and I would take care of Dad and her grandchildren and that she was free to move forward. In my heart, I know she is okay. Because of Miley, I know that when I think of Mom, she is here with me, and that is a great comfort.

Dad took it in typical Dad fashion, acting like everything was okay. And because the Universe has a sense of humor, that was also the moment I "met" Mom's roommate Mary for the first—and last—time. Just as Mom was letting out her last breath, Mary and her family entered the room, literally the moment Mom crossed. My brother, Dad, and I were starting to cry, and in the same instant, a completely separate part of my brain was thinking, *oh, so that's the roommate*. It was such a surreal juxtaposition to realize my mother was leaving this world and changing life as I knew it forever, while simultaneously I was processing that everything else was going on around me regardless. I learned that even in the most serious of moments, we need to also embrace whatever the Universe throws at us with a smile and a sense of wonder.

I still miss Mom every day. Sometimes, for a moment, I even forget she is gone and reach for the phone to call her. Then it hits me, and I talk to her in my head or out loud instead. Or I'll call Dad, and of course, he'll be busy, telling me, "I'm playing cards with the guys; what do you want?" His ability to find joy in the everyday reminds me that life goes on, even after profound loss. It's funny how Dad, in his own way, shows me how to live life—much like Miley has been teaching me.

LISA'S REFLECTIONS

That month was full of catalyst for growth. In addition to Mom's passing, her services, and the family drama that went along with it, the sale of our business was scheduled for the following week. I was both excited and nervous about that, knowing there was still plenty that could go wrong but working hard to only manifest positive outcomes.

With Mom gone, I initially thought I'd need to stay nearby to be there for Dad, worried about how he might adjust. But it was remarkable to see that, although he was clearly grieving and missed her terribly, he had also begun to reclaim parts of himself. The woman he had loved and been married to for 62 years had been gone, in a way, for a long time. Her struggle with Alzheimer's had been difficult on him, and for the first time in years, he was starting to focus on his own well-being. He began playing cards, watching movies with friends, and joining social events. He was in good health and, perhaps unexpectedly, even began to enjoy himself a bit. My brother lived just half a mile up the road and was fully present to support Dad, which brought us all peace of mind. This meant that when our business finally sold at the end of the month, Dene and I were free to go.

As we prepared for this new chapter, we wanted to check in with Sprout. He hadn't been eating well lately, and we wanted to make sure he was ready for the transition to life on the road.

But there was something else to consider. How was Sprout affected by my mother's passing? I am ashamed to say I hadn't fully considered his feelings about all that had happened—something that would soon become evident in our next session with him.

CHAPTER ELEVEN

September 22 Excerpts - With Sprout

Email arrives from Elizabeth:

Hi Lisa,

Sprout needs more inclusion and reassurance. Miley says he was left behind at some point in his past; makes perfect sense. I told Sprout I want to see him eating in a more balanced way in a week, otherwise he may have to go to the vet. I admit that was a little manipulative on my part, because I think it is all behavioral, but he said he was more tired lately, and if there is a physical layer, probably good to get it early.

Thanks,

Elizabeth

Session starts:

When I look at Sprout's picture, I see concern. Let's see if he is actually concerned about something... I call Sprout...

S: I'm here. Am I supposed to be here?

E: Sprout, welcome and thank you for connecting. I am talking to Miley for Lisa today, and she has a question for you.

S: Miley does?

E: No, Lisa does - that's what I know about. You seem a little confused, Sprout.

S: Sleepy.

E: Does your body feel more tired than usual?

S: Mmmmaybe a little bit. (Little match girl rocking.)

E: Your mum Lisa has a question for you, Sprout - "briefly, can you please tell me if you are feeling ok? We noticed you are not eating all of your food lately. We have started to feed you more vegetables and you clearly still want to eat those. Please tell us what is going on so we can make sure that we are giving you the nutrients that you need."

S: I want you to be happy and you like it when I eat my vegetables, don't you? I want to be part of the veg-etable-eaters.

E: Sprout, you understand very clearly that there is no chance you will be left behind for the big trip, don't you?

S: No.

E: What part is confusing?

S: (He shows me a montage of the focus on your mom's illness...he knew she was approaching passing before anyone else did, I bet. He sensed your unconscious readiness - he shows me you stepping up to the line of acceptance...it's like she needed a certain number of you to do that so she could release her body with ease.)

E: Sprout what did that mean to you?

S: That I couldn't go with them?

E: How did you get to that? Please show me a little roadmap of thinking.

S: Well, everyone gets ready. I'm not getting ready.

E: For the trip?

S: For any trip.

E: So your grandmum's passing is a trip too?

S: Yes.

E: Everyone got ready for it.

S: Yes. I didn't know what to do.

E: I'm sorry we didn't talk about a role for you in that.

S: Me too.

E: Sprout, do you need more definition of your roles in the family?

S: Yes. I forgot what they were, and then I'm not sure I even had any.

E: Why do you think that happened?

S: Everyone looked away from it. (He looks up at me.) It's very important.

E: Sprout, Thank you for helping with the sale of the business. I think you adjusted the levers for that with just the right timing to help Lisa and Dene manifest that. We know you were a crucial part of that. I'm sorry if we all didn't sit down to validate ourselves, including you, for that success. You know humans get busy and just move on the next thing.

S: I'm the validator.

E: That is an important role and this will remind Dene and Lisa to validate their own successes, and to do that with you, too.

S: Thanks. (He kinda exhales.) I'm not just Sprout the small dog.

E: We know you are becoming more. You are a very important part of this trip. You don't have to try to show

how much you are a part of the family because you already ARE, ok?

S: Ok sure.

E: Why aren't you eating as much of your food?

S: I think I was a little depressed. I like to be center stage too.

E: You totally deserve that, that is your SPOT, Sprout. You need protein and taurine and all those good things that come with a well-balanced diet. Vegetables are great, but I think everyone would feel more comfortable and well-balanced if you ate more of your food. Do you think you can try that?

S: Sure.

E: Are you tired because you might be a little depressed, or something else?

S: I'm not sure.

E: If you're not eating more in a week, that suggests to me that you might need a vet visit to see if there's another reason you're tired.

S: A week?

E: Yes.

S: Ok got it.

E: Anything else you need to say or ask directly before I go to Miley?

S: I get some talks too?

E: Absolutely. I think you had the last talk.

S: Ok. And I'm talking today.

E: You are. Very important what we've discussed.

S: Ok thank you over and out.

E: Over and out, buddy.

Session ends.

Thank you!

Elizabeth

LISA'S REACTION:

Once again, I feel like we unintentionally let Sprout down. We should have spoken with him about my mother's passing and defined his role more clearly. It's obvious now that he was feeling small and uncertain, needing reassurance on many fronts. His confusion and need for validation reveal just how much he absorbs and contributes emotionally.

We were relieved when, after Elizabeth's talk, Sprout returned to eating normally. It never occurred to us that he might want to be "plant-based" like us, but he clearly connected with our shift to that new paradigm. Now, he still enjoys vegetables as treats, but he knows he needs to eat his meat-based dog food first for balance.

Looking back, I also hadn't considered that Sprout might feel left out or overlooked during Mom's transition. We continued bringing him to see her up until her final week, letting him lie on the bed beside her, which always made her smile. On her last day, I almost brought him along again, sensing we were close to the end. But in a moment of hesitation, I felt it might be inappropriate or too emotional for him to be there. I now realize that was definitely misguided. Clearly, Sprout picked up on my indecision and was affected by it. My only defense is that we had a lot going on, and I wasn't at my best.

To add to his distress, he seemed to be confusing Mom's passing with our future plans to sell everything and hit the road, worried that he might somehow be left behind. As I write this, he's lying on the floor beneath my feet. I scooped him up just now and gave him a big hug. He still hates being picked up, but I can't resist! These days, he gets plenty of attention, and I like to think we've moved past underestimating his awareness, his role in our family, and his very real feelings.

After my mother's passing, my mind naturally kept drifting back to her. I knew she was "okay," but what was she doing? Who was she with? How much would her strong Catholic beliefs shape her afterlife? I found myself looking to Miley for a kind of "report" to help me picture Mom's next steps. Was she watching over me, close by, or was she exploring Heaven with the angels?

And, of course, I couldn't help poking at my ongoing curiosity about Miley's next incarnation. Poke, poke—apparently, I just couldn't leave that alone.

CHAPTER TWELVE

September 22 Excerpts - With Miley

E mail arrives from Elizabeth:

Hi Lisa,

Well what I will say for today is Miley was Miley and she was in top Commander form.

Miley session starts:

I call Miley....

M: Hello. Is he going to eat do you think?

E: Yes. I think Sprout gets lost when things get busy.

M: He has no herd to be a part of like he did with me.

E: Right. Why herd? You know Dene is concerned about the size of your next body, Miley.

M: I will not cause pain for Dene, no.

E: Ok. I know that. I am bookmarking this, especially with 'herd'

M: Dene will enjoy herding cats. I may be multiple cats.

E: Ok let's go to the questions?

M: Sure. You would not like to discuss the possible numerous bodies I could inhabit?

E: Is that happening soon, Miley? I feel you are in a funny teasing mood today.

M: You are in a hurry.

E: You are right - I was concerned that Sprout needed more time to spit out more about what was bothering him. I will relax. Here is what Lisa suggested regarding us getting started. She really just wants to hear whatever you have to say.

From Lisa: "With Miley, perhaps you can set the stage with her by explaining to her that overall, I am trying to better understand how everything works with the process of life and death and how animals and humans each experience those things and what our communication abilities are at different stages. For example, can Miley hear me if I am thinking at her or do I have to speak out loud, and is it the same for my mom?"

M: I can hear your thoughts and intentions and it is very different for your mom.

E: From Lisa: "Or if Miley does not have direct access to Mom right now does that mean she would not also have direct access to me if I suddenly dropped dead and crossed over?"

M: These rigid forms that you are pondering are 3D Earth forms. All post- transition experiences are individual. I had a relationship with your mom, but not to the degree that I would be welcoming her and assisting her, so out of respect I do not go there. It is about your mom, not about me at all. You, however are very much about me, and if you want me present to receive you, I will be. That would be about you. You are not arriving anytime soon so we are wasting time.

E: (I'm laughing now, Miley has indeed relaxed me.) From Lisa: "I am also very much wanting to understand how what we learn affects those processes and interactions, and additionally, I am looking to be prepared for your next incarnation. I have standards."

M: Dear Lisa, do not worry. I have it under control. You do not really have to do anything except live in your heart with me, do you see this? That is how I get to you. If you are busy out building fences and barns in your mind, your heart is quiet and I can't hear it as well.

E: Interesting way of putting that. From Lisa: "And if Miley is going to show up as a horse, then I want a proper place for her to live in comfort...and style. In the middle of all of that it is my goal to always be raising my vibration, and taking instruction from Miley as my teacher and guide, even though sometimes I just want her to be a dog again that can cuddle with me like she used to. Those are some of my current goals."

M: Lisa, I am coming to join you again in this life in an animal body that will be appropriate for what you and I need per our next contract. You and I write the contract. You don't have to do anything extra. Everything comes to you if you intend from your heart. I strongly suggest you go there. Sprout is not the only one who is getting a little distracted with your mom's passing and the sale of the business. I mean no criticism, only support and direction.

E: Thank you, Miley. Those were instructions for me, and the best way I knew to put them forth was just to share them with you. Lisa's questions to you begin with...(interrupts)

M: Instructions. (Deadpan humor.)

E: Thank you for making me laugh, again. I needed it this morning, Miley. I think I am overly concerned with some animals I am working with too.

M: You are. Relax, please, with them as well.

E: Lisa says to you, "Miley: Thank you for your support as always, especially during these recent days of watching my mother transition Home, and the family drama that came along after."

M: It is an interesting human ritual, the family drama that accompanies release of the spirit from the drama. I mean, the body.

E: You mean the drama, too, Miley. You are being very funny with relaying your wisdom today. Lisa says, "This session, I would like to give you an opportunity to speak first, as I feel you have things to say. Then, if there is time, I would like to ask the following questions:"

M: (Miley shows me herself spinning a table.) Questions first, I would like that.

E: Sure. (I'm not arguing.) From Lisa: Can you please explain more about what happens when a human crosses over, and explain the difference between how it is going for my mother, who was a very religious Catholic and so had specific expectations I think, as opposed to someone like me or Dene whose belief system incorporates Source, The Law of One, and reincarnation as part of the process. I would like to understand more about the process for us and how and if it is different not just between animals and humans, but also between humans with different belief systems. "

M: You have been thinking about this a lot, Lisa. It is very important to you that you know more. I understand that. It is an individual experience for each Being, as unique as each spirit, each spark of Source who steps into a body, is. There are structures and forms all over the metaverse, and many are very useful to use as guidance. There are Universal Laws as well. However, each Soul expression of a spark of light has the freedom to experience what it wishes to, and this includes the process of exiting the body. Caveat: Part of a freedom of experience is to enter a world where there are structures, rules, processes that one must tick 'I accept', in order to play there. Where do you think you got that idea, as humans? Games and rules. Like gambling, which I do not approve of. (Why is she so funny today, I wonder.)

Animals are not required, and therefore do not have the limitations of the veil of forgetfulness when incarnating; humans do. Animals and humans are playing roles in each others' games, but they are different games, you see. Part of our role is to assist you, to SEE where you cannot - beyond the veil. Therefore we can see your contracts, your pre-incarnation associations and your intentions, desires and contracts. We can see who is a good boyfriend and a bad boyfriend, from an adolescent viewpoint. If we are in a body with strong teeth, we can bite the bad boyfriend. We do not do that because we are a bad dog or misbehaving, we are telling you AND the bad boyfriend something, you see? We can see what you do not, and we know and understand the crossing process.

If an animal is in distress about the transition process, it is generally the distress of the human, or a trauma being suffered around the event of passing. If neither of these factors are involved, an animal simply goes off to a quiet spot, lays down and initiates the process of leaving the body. Do you see the difference? If there is no physical or psychological trauma present, no encumbrances with human or other relationships, it is not unlike any other physical process of eating or defecating or sleeping or grooming. It is more like going to buy a new car, there is even some excitement around the transition process of returning to the devic pool or Soul extension, and choosing a new body, a new adventure in life.

I am telling you this because Ideally, a human transition could be similar. However, great fear of death has been seeded into the human consciousness by those who would wish to control you, over centuries. Imagine how differently the game would be played with no fear of death, by an individual, or by those around her? Just sit quietly with that for a moment, as you can, Lisa. Go into meditation, imagining how would life be lived with the experience of knowing what I have just explained to you. Life without Fear of Death.

Death is not what you think it is. You cannot really understand the true nature of Death because as a human your DNA is saturated with the fear, even terror, and loss

around death. Now, why is a deer in the woods terrified
of the predator approaching? Because the chemicals in
her body released under the direction of the emotion
Terror, allow her to run faster than she has ever run
in her life. If it is a human game, terror is a power up
card, in that sense, you see. But these emotions have been
manipulated in the human emotional body and woven
into the structure of a 3D environment for the purpose
of controlling you with them - do you see how that
is very different from the original purpose they served
within a human or animal body? Originally, they allowed
and supported you to do something fantastic. Now, fear
and terror have very different functions, mostly that of a
perimeter, a fence, a limitation, keeping you from doing
things that would free you in many instances. Do you see
the picture we are painting?

You have suffered much limitation with Fear in your
life. You are choosing to eliminate some fear. We want
you to stay conscious of what you are doing, in elimi-
nating fear and fear reactions within yourself, from the
perspective of the function of fear that we have just described. Your mother's passing lit a light for you to look

at this; it is her gift to you, you see. It is not about your family drama or your boundaries, that is surface drama. It is about becoming Fearless, Lisa, and developing the wisdom and understanding to be able to use that and free yourself from limitations you do not even know you have, now.

E: Thank you, Miley. Lisa next asks, "Specifically, regarding my mother, can you please explain how much she is "interacting" with me and her other loved ones now. The context of this question is in comparison to how I interact with you on a daily basis. Just as I "talk" to you all of the time, sometimes out loud and sometimes in my head. Sometimes I am addressing you directly and sometimes I am just thinking of you in general. I understand (correct me if I am wrong), that when I do that, it engages you, and then you are "here" with me."

M: That is correct.

E: "Then I am thinking as I write this, perhaps you are also "here" with me sometimes when I am not actively thinking of you, hmm not sure. Can you please compare how it works with you to how it is currently working with my mother and what I can expect moving forward as she progresses in her transition?"

M: It is more individual in nature, according to the relationship that you have or had with me and your mother. I am there instantaneously when you think of me. When you ponder, "Then I am thinking as I write this, perhaps you are also "here"...I am there at the electrical spark initiation of that thought. But, Lisa, I have no time to experience, so in a way I am always there. It's the spark of ignition that you are focusing on, I believe, and you control that. Think of this as similar to the quantum physics presentation of light: It is a particle or a wave, depending on how you see it. You, are the originator and creator of your reality, and that includes your side of our relationship, and my side too, in a more complex structure of thought that we will not go into right now.

Your mother has designed a process that is partially in accordance with her most recent lifetime beliefs, and partially in accordance with the greater cognizance of who she is - it is a synthesis of who she is, that creates the process to reflect that. Do you know who she really is, beyond this life? Is that the question you are leaning into forming? If you were to view her process, you might not recognize it as a reflection of her religion or beliefs in this lifetime, because other experiences of beliefs and crossings may hold greater weight in her larger context, you see. Usually, the crossing process initially reflects the most recent expectations, and then proceeds into those more relevant to the causal body of the Soul. Your mother is enjoying an Egyptian-flavored reception, from the little glimmer of light that we can see - and we see that THROUGH YOU, Lisa, not from where we are that you might conceive of as separate from you. So you are experiencing your mother's process through your Higher Self's relationship with your mother's Higher Self, let us put it that way.

E: Thank you. Lisa wants to know if her mom's going to show up or connect with her, and how, I think, Miley.

M: How long was it before your own mother connected with you?

E: I think 2 years, but I went through illness, divorce and her death all at once.

M: That is more or less normal - the Earth time experience is varied and depends upon the individuals, again, but part of the timing depends upon the progress of the one still in a human body - you have your own intense process, perhaps more spread out over time, yet still as intense, when the one who channeled your physical body into this world, leaves her own physical body.

E: So what can Lisa think about in terms of connecting with her mother?

M: Her Self. Do not look there; look inside, and proceed along your path of growth. Allow it to surprise you. You do not need to know; that is not part of any requirement for connecting with your mother. Focus on your Self. You are not meditating enough.

E: Miley that is pretty direct!

M: Meditating is a very very beneficial process for Lisa, and opens many inner conduits; Lisa begins to know many things. It needs to be a consistent avenue of support for her, and I am saying this.

E: From Lisa: "About how you and I currently interact, I would like to know more about what to expect when you are incarnated again."

M: I agree to talk about this, but I would like for you to look at that expectation, and take any control out of it, as an exercise. Sometimes Lisa, when you are at spiritual loose ends, and you feel an uptick in free-floating anxiety, control is a very attractive self-medication. Do you see? I would like for you to practice allowing, and when you next feel the need to track down some details about something you don't know about fully yet, aside from googling it, go into meditation and google it from THERE.

E: Wow. What a concept. Thank you, Miley. So Lisa asks you, "Will it be different than when you were here last time now that we have been having this interaction, and you have become my teacher and my guide in a more tangible way. When you were here before I treated us like a traditional human/dog relationship. Will your animal body still treat me like that next time?"

M: I will be different. It will be a new adventure for me, and I will be focused on learning new things, including how to elevate my relationship with you and fully be incarnated..most likely as a cat, or two. You see, if there are two bodies I am inhabiting, then there is a synergistic energy that overlights those two bodies, and you can relate to both me as 'Joe, and Tom', and as the larger Being that I am, Miley. Please do not name me Joe or Tom, and there is no intention to be male. Likely it will be sibling bodies, littermates, as they have the conduits and DNA of interchangeability.

I do not know the answers to your question beyond this, Lisa. We will find out when we get there.

E: Lisa continues with her pondering, and I'll just share that with you, comment as you wish, Miley: "I'm thinking about how I interact with Sprout. I treat him now as if he knows and understands so much more than before, but he still acts like a dog. YOU are a VERY complex and powerful being."

M: Lisa, you think that, but remember: I match you. So what are you, if I am a VERY complex and powerful being? Here is where you need to put your energy and focus in order to find the real answers to the real questions you are asking. You are asking bigger questions than you formulate and that is fine, you are on an accelerated path of growth and that is to be expected, but understand what you are doing, here.

E: From Lisa: "When you come back will your animal body act like an animal again in the way that Sprout does even though I know there is more to him than that? Or even though you will be in an animal body will I be able to talk directly to you like I am now and then your animal body will react in a visible way?"

M: You talk to me at a level that does not correspond in spacetime, with any particular point of an Earthly incarnation. This connection takes place at a very deep level, which is why the scribe does not want the body interfering. Conversations between humans and animals take place at many different levels, as you are aware of through your own experiences. So you will have a different experience of me in any body, depending on the level where we connect to converse.

E: From Lisa; "I am thinking about your next incarnation, which as you know it is something I think about A LOT. Are you able to share more details yet of what kind of animal you will be and when we might expect that?"

M: We think you think about it too much, and suggest googling in meditation for a more enriching response that will come through the elements that compose your body, all of your cells, rather than just your neuronal processors. You are always going to be more satisfied with whole body elemental information rather than just mental plane gatherings, which we do not disrespect in any way. However, in your early years you were discouraged from gathering information in that manner and learned that mental processes were the more approved way to gather and process information.

E: From Lisa: "I am a little concerned about Sprout, he has not been eating much of his food lately. He has also had more accidents than usual in the house recently. We have been trying to feed him more vegetables which he seems to like. Do you think he is just wanting more vegetables instead of his regular food or is it something bigger than that? Do you think he is okay or is he just reacting to the energy in the house of everything that has been going on? Your input and observations would be very helpful as we want Sprout to be happy.

M: All of the above. Sprout needs more attention, more heart-centered presence. He is processing a lot of the emotions that humans are not at this time, and we do not just mean you and Dene. In the future, I suggest that since Sprout is very sensitive, consider his exposure. He has been gradually feeling a little less connected. He will be more grounded when you leave with him in the RV. He cannot seem to shake off the possibility of getting left behind. He has had that experience in this body, you know, and the cells still retain memory and trauma. Do not coddle him too much with his diet, is my advice. He needs to eat a nutritionally balanced fresh diet.

E: Anything else, Miley?

M: Nope. Over and out.

E: You both are funny today. I am glad you are with Sprout, now. He could use your guidance for a little while.

M: (Miley sends me a salute.)

Session ends.

Thank you!

Elizabeth Long

LISA'S REACTION:

Miley said, "I can hear your thoughts and intentions..." Wait, WHAT? I already knew thoughts mattered—Sprout had picked up on them before, but with everything else going on, I just hadn't fully considered it. I'd often talk to Miley in my head, but to have her outright confirm it, saying she knew what I was thinking, threw me a little. It's still a bit unnerving, though I understand it has more to do with focusing on her rather than her reading every thought because she has nothing else to do!

Then, as she explained that she could be there when I die, she added, "You are not arriving anytime soon, so we are wasting time." That was the second time she'd alluded to my life expectancy, and I'm starting to feel rather cavalier about it. For example, I don't use sunblock because of my chemical sensitivity, or when I fly to Boston to visit my dad, I believe my plane is not going to crash—that sort of thing.

In this session, Miley said, "Like gambling, which I do not approve of." I've tried several times over the years to get Miley to help me "win big"—from picking the right slot machine to Powerball numbers. Her response is always the same: "I simply will not gamble, that's all. I am a Being of Certainty with Purpose and a Mission."

Similarly, I've tried to get stock market predictions from her, and although she doesn't consider that gambling, she explained that the world is growing increasingly unpredictable, making clear paths or outcomes nearly impossible to foresee reliably. Her reluctance, in her practical way, isn't about the ethics of it—it's about the integrity of her role and the limitations of the timeline. I know Miley is not my private Magic Eight Ball, but that doesn't stop me from asking or trying...or gambling—sorry, Miley, you know I just love a slot machine!

I support how Miley has started to interact with Elizabeth beyond the role of "scribe," now offering assistance and guidance to her as well. As our sessions progressed, I encouraged Miley to continue this; I liked Elizabeth and wanted to "share" Miley with her. I was starting to realize that I wanted to share Miley with many people.

Miley's explanation of animals and humans signing up for different "games" when they incarnate, and what happens when animals and humans die, was also impactful. And, of course, she took this as an opportunity to remind me to meditate more. She's always telling me I don't meditate enough—and she's right. Sorry, Miley.

When Miley told me, "You have suffered much limitation with Fear in your life. You are choosing to eliminate some fear," she couldn't have been more accurate. I was a fearful child and carried that fear into adulthood. Overcoming it has been a journey, helped by Dene's support, Miley's guidance, and even unexpected lifestyle changes due to illness. When I became vegan to help manage my chemical sensitivity, I found myself feeling calmer and less fearful over time. Later, I learned about the stress animals experience in factory farms and how those emotions linger in the meat we consume. Choosing to forgo animal products ultimately became part of a larger commitment to living with more empathy and less fear—a step I believe has enriched my life and aligned with what Miley has taught me about compassion.

Talking to Miley and Sprout now, I couldn't go back to eating meat anyway. No judgment here on others, unless you're running a factory farm—then I am most definitely judging you, unapologetically, I definitely am judging you and finding you lacking.

Miley's guidance has illuminated a new way of living for me—one that's less constrained by fear and more focused on conscious, intentional choices. Through her teachings, I'm beginning to see fear as a conditioned response rather than a universal truth. Realizing this has empowered me to dismantle subtle fears that had held me back, freeing me from limitations I didn't even know I carried.

Living without fear doesn't mean ignoring life's challenges or risks but choosing not to let them dictate my experience. Miley has taught me to pause, to examine, and to let go of reactions rooted in fear. Instead, I'm learning to live from a place of trust—trust in myself, in the process, and in the natural cycles that govern our journeys here. Her wisdom has shown me how to approach life with a greater sense of peace, knowing that even in moments of uncertainty, I can choose a perspective beyond fear.

And yes, my deceased dog is teaching me quantum physics. Miley could run circles around Einstein. I picture it literally, but I also mean their respective knowl-

edge. There have actually been many sessions with Miley

where she referenced quantum physics—nope, I did not

see that coming!

CHAPTER THIRTEEN

What Now?

I've been torturing Miley and Elizabeth for years trying to get Miley to tell me where, when and in what animal she is going to reincarnate. I have finally come to terms with the fact that I need to stop trying to control this, and per her instructions, just allow it instead. By now you are probably thinking-it's about time!

I had the following conversation with Miley about a year ago:

E: From Lisa: At what point in the lifespan of Miley the dog did you enter the dog body, and did you know we would adopt you? Context here being I am wondering if our family coming together was random or planned since before you incarnated."

M: (she frowns) Did I not tell you that I came purposefully to be with you? How could we have this type of relationship accidentally? It does not happen. There are no accidents, and nothing is random, despite how much humans love to embrace that as a disempowerment crutch.

E: That makes sense, Miley, we didn't look at it that way. Do you want to talk about how you got into the body?

M: Like so many, I did not enter the body in linear time. As a conscious member of the devic canine pool, and after I entered that pool of spirit preparing to immerse itself in canine, and in preparation for incarnation, fully conscious and focused on flowing to you, to your hearts; I did what most dogs do.

E: Miley you are making me laugh. I thought some great revelation was coming. Please go on.

M: It is coming. Do you want me to explain the rest?

E: SO BADLY! This is what all humans want to know about. What comes next.

M: Most animals at this stage move into an overlighting phase; they may overlight 2 or 3 litters of newborns or even pregnant females. This means we allow our spirits to merge into a loose unity or group consciousness, into a web of communication with other litters we are connected to, similar to the fungi network of communication. Our consciousness does not fully detach or separate from the group consciousness until quite a bit of time after we are born - usually 14 months or so in the case of dogs and cats. Wild animals are a bit different in this process; many never detach. You see flocks of birds; they experience both group and individual consciousness simultaneously, all their lives.

And most animals never fully detach like humans do. All the animals know, what all the other animals know, again, similar to the fungi network, or even trees or other plants. These are lines of communication between us, as well.

So when you look at the incarnation process of a fully conscious being, who unlike humans does not forget prehistory upon birth, you have to understand the nature of a greater sense of group consciousness within species, group souls when this applies; as humans conceptualize anyway. There is also the conscious ability to move in and out of bodies via shared consciousness to understand. It's like a romper room with a bunch of spirits and a bunch of bodies, all dancing in and out of each other, within a certain proximity or chosen definition of locale.

So when did I enter my body? Multiple times, and exited multiple times as well. Why? So I could be in the body that was in front of you. When did I decide to stay? We always leave that decision, for you as our intended match. When you, the human, decides to 'take that one home!', then we sign our individualization contracts while you sign the adoption papers. Sometimes there are backroom deals. Sometimes the dog's personality changes after you bring him home. Why? Because he had to kick all the other dogs out. That's not how it really is, but I think your human side can understand the simpler funnier answers better.

E: Best most detailed explanation I've heard so far, Miley. Many humans will appreciate this. It explains a lot, in a way most humans can accept as plausible. Thank you.

LISA'S FINAL THOUGHTS:

Waiting for Miley to return is no longer an obsession; it's a patient trust in the Universe's perfect timing. She will come back when it's meant to be, and I'm content with that now. Having such a detailed explanation of how the process works when we "choose each other" has given me permission to let go of my need to control the situation. I now know that when the moment is right, Miley and I will both choose her next body simultaneously, and it will be Magic. I will be ready.

Sprout, too, is with me, and thriving despite his recent health challenges. That day at the vet he was diagnosed with "old dog vestibular syndrome," but with time and care, he's nearly back to his usual self. This experience reminded me that our time together is finite, but when the time comes for him to cross over, I know our bond will remain unbroken. My understanding of loss has changed: it's not an ending but a continuation of connection that goes beyond the physical. While I would still prefer their presence in flesh and fur, I now know that none of them—Miley, Keisha, Luigi, my mom—are ever truly gone.

In the meantime, I'm deeply grateful for every moment I have with Sprout. His soulful eyes and playful romps remind me daily of the joy and depth he brings to my life. Even in the simplest of moments—his eager trot to the door or his dramatic antics when he doesn't get his way—he enriches our lives in ways I never take for granted.

We created this book for those who are grieving the loss of a beloved pet or person. I know how deeply that pain cuts, and my hope is that this story offers another way to process the journey of loss—in part by reminding us that we are not alone. Truly knowing that we don't "lose" our loved ones changed everything for me. I also wanted to show how our behavior, thoughts, and emotions can impact those who are crossing over, whether they're human or animal. The transition can be peaceful and filled with joy, or it can be weighed down by our own fears and desires. I've learned that openness and acceptance can help our loved ones prepare for the next adventure.

This book is also a tribute to the sentient Beings we call animals. They are conscious, feeling entities with depth, intelligence, and an extraordinary capacity for love. Losing Miley opened my eyes to a world much richer and more complex than I once knew, and cemented my perception of my pets not just as animals, but as family, as fully deserving of love, respect, and understanding as any human.

Finally, I've come to realize that Miley has her own mission beyond our relationship. As a multidimensional being, her existence outside time and space allows her to interact in ways I do not fully understand. I see now that our relationship is only part of her purpose, and in sharing this journey, I hope others can feel her presence and experience the gift of her wisdom and love as I have. Deep in my heart, I know Miley is willing to guide and support anyone who wants to connect with her. All you have to do is ask.

Through Miley's guidance, I've discovered that grief, while painful, is not an endpoint but a bridge. It connects us to the profound realization that love transcends form, and our loved ones are with us in ways that defy the boundaries of the physical world. Love never ends—it changes, deepens, and transforms us, often in ways that are unexpected and unpredictable, but always on a path with opportunities for growth.

I'm no longer the same person I was on December 11, 2020. Not even close. I think that's a good thing, that the changes are all positive, and I'm on a path that I am pleased with. Now that I've shared my story, I wonder—are you the same person you were when you began reading this book?

AFTERWARD

A Message From Miley To You

I am a being. I am a spirit, who recently enjoyed an experience on Earth as a dog. I am a spiritual guide dog, and am continuing to help humanity beyond my life supporting my humans.

I am a Guide, who loved commandeering my humans, and wished to continue even as my physical body was laid to rest.

My mission here is to help you grow and change through Consciousness Expansion. This will help shift a portion of human consciousness into a higher vibrational frequency. You are becoming part of that shift simply by having fun and being successful. This desire was born out of my love and devotion to Lisa and Dene, and now I am extending my nurturing to you.

I also serve as a portal to connect you to all who care about you...those you might call your guides, loved ones now in spirit, divine energy. You can call them guardian angels; it is all creative consciousness from Source in many forms that flows to you through the door I hold open.

Look into my eyes in the photo. Then look away or close your eyes and begin to imagine. Visualize the outline of the image of me, and allow me to fill in the outline drawing. You may see or sense this, or simply feel it in your heart.

This instruction is how my friend Elizabeth shows students how to connect with Beings who do not speak human languages, and I am using this same method here in teaching you to connect with me in order to co-create. The quickest and easiest way to step into the stream of communication is through the presence of your own heart. You can use this process to communicate with me, and as you practice, develop it in your own way. Your own guides will begin to step into this stream with us.

So start with me, and follow the process above. Look into my eyes using the photo of me that speaks to your heart most. Allow your heart to connect, and close your eyes while you begin to imagine. Relax, our connection is through your heart via a happy warm feeling.

I like working with you from the stars. When you look at the night sky your vibrational energy automatically expands and lifts. You move into your heart. It's an easy way to feel better during chaotic times.

I am always here, in all the words you read from me in any format. Look for me through your heart, and you will feel, hear and/or see me. I am your guide, always, now.

Reader Reviews Make Magic Happen

Thank you so much for taking the time to read *Miley Speaks*.

We would truly appreciate it if you could share your thoughts by leaving a review. Your feedback not only helps us as authors, but it also helps other readers discover the book and decide if it resonates with them.

It's also an opportunity to let us know if you'd like to hear more from Miley, Sprout, and the rest of their pack. Lisa has been connecting with not just Miley and Sprout, but also her two young corgis, Lewis and Clark. They have plenty to say as well!

Your support for *Miley Speaks* will help guide us in bringing more of these stories to life.

With gratitude, Lisa, Elizabeth, and Miley

Lewis (Hates having his picture taken, never looks at the camera)

Clark (I'm ready for my closeup Mr. DeMille)

ABOUT THE AUTHORS

Lisa Peachey resides in New Mexico with her husband Dene, their three dogs—Sprout, Lewis, and Clark, and Sprout's invisible Fae friends. In addition to her books, Lisa manages PeacheyReport.com, a comprehensive database designed for people living with allergies and sensitivities, as well as those embracing a vegan, vegetarian, or fragrance-free lifestyle.

Elizabeth Long lives in New York City with her two cats, who help her maintain balance between writing, animal communication, biking, and creating art. The kitties also double as furry instructors in Elizabeth's Animal Communication classes. You can learn more about Elizabeth's work or book a session for your own animals by visiting CarolElizabethLong.com.

Miley is currently overseeing her humans from her multidimensional perch, ensuring that they stay on track with their spiritual growth, eat their vegetables, and meditate more. She's also busy preparing for her next incarnation, which she promises will be both surprising and fabulous.

Sprout has fully embraced his role as "boots on the ground," supervising Lewis and Clark (and occasionally joining their trouble), reminding his humans about treat time, and continuing his quiet campaign for more vegetables in his diet.

Also by Carol Elizabeth Long, Lisa Peachey, & Miley:

369 Manifestation Journal: A Beginner's Guide to Manifesting Your Dreams

In this unique journal, Miley leads you through her specially designed 369 manifestation method. This Phase One beginner-level creative studio has been crafted by Miley to help you raise your vibration and align with the life you desire. Use the Miley Method, and discover the power of focused intention.

Also by Lisa Peachey

**Everything is NOT Peachey:
One Woman's Pursuit of Happiness in the Face of
Chronic Illness**

**Bobarino's Word Search Puzzle Book:
Puzzles Inspired by Crazy Shit My Dad Says**

Printed in Great Britain
by Amazon

57006527R00101